Carmel in the World Paperbacks
16

**CARMEL
SCHOOL OF PRAYER**

JOSEPH CHALMERS, O. CARM.

Carmel
School of Prayer

EDIZIONI CARMELITANE

ROMA

Cover: *Prayer at night*
photo: mrehan

© Edizioni Carmelitane 2010

ISBN: 978-88-7288-114-9
IT ISSN: 0394-7750

EDIZIONI CARMELITANE
via Sforza Pallavicini, 10
00193 Roma, Italia
edizioni@ocarm.org

*Finito di stampare nel mese di maggio 2010
dalla Tipografia Abilgraph srl – Roma*

TABLE OF CONTENTS

Preface	3
Carmel: The Future	7
Carmelites and the Future	21
Carmel and Hope	31
Carmelite Prayer: Source of Energy	45
Carmel: A Light in the Darkness	75
Contemplation and the Carmelite Rule	109
The God of our Contemplation	141
St. Thérèse of Lisieux for the Third Millennium	173
Mary Obedient to the Word	195
The Future of Our Past: The Scapular for the Third Millennium	217
The Lord Hears the Cry of the Poor	231
Our Mendicant Tradition	267

PREFACE

The following chapters of this book began life as individual talks or letters given during the second term of Fr. Joseph Chalmers as Prior General (2001-2007). They have been edited and re-worked to fit into a book format. Some of the chapters are directed more specifically towards lay Carmelites while others have Carmelite religious in view. There is a certain amount of overlap of course. As much as possible inclusive language has been used. This is particularly so in the horizontal dimension but not so much in the vertical, i.e. in the relationship that God has with us. The author draws a line at using "God gives Godself" or any such phrase. If any offence is given by this decision, a heartfelt apology is offered.

The first chapters look towards the future and see in Carmel many reasons for hope. Above all Carmel is seen as a school of prayer and its long tradition is viewed with an eye to the future.

Whatever our image of God, Carmelite spirituality is directed towards purifying our image of God and every aspect of our lives so that we might be what God has created each one of us to be.

The biblical quotes throughout the book are taken from a variety of translations, usually either from the *New Revised Standard Version* (1989) or the *New American Bible* (Thomas Nelson Inc., New Jersey, 1971)

CARMEL. THE FUTURE

What will the future hold? If we knew that, we could all make a fortune. We are invited into God's future and only He knows what that will be but He is constructing the future out of our present. We are laying the foundations now for what we will be in the future. I would like now to share with you some dreams I have for the future of Carmel and how I see lay Carmelites in particular fitting into that future.

Karl Rahner said that the Christian of the future will be a mystic. Many people seem to want to settle for far less than they were created for. Even church people can succumb to that temptation. However you want more. The fact that you are Carmelites and that you are taking the time to read this means that you are seeking more. But what is this more?

In the future of the Church I see the goal of Christianity being spelled out much more clearly and I believe that Carmel has a very important role to play in this future. The goal of Christianity is not just to say your prayers and avoid mortal sin so that you will get to heaven after passing through purgatory. I think that the goal is nowhere better expressed than in the letter to the Ephesians:

> *This then is what I pray, kneeling before the Father from whom every family whether spiritual or natural takes its*

name, that out of His infinite glory He may grant you the power, through His Spirit, for your hidden self to grow strong so that Christ may live in your hearts through faith and then planted in love and built on love, you will with all the saints have strength to grasp the breadth and the length, the height and the depth; until knowing the love of Christ which is beyond all knowledge, you are filled with the utter fullness of God. Glory be to Him who wants to do far more for us than we could ask for or even imagine. Glory be to Him in the Church and in Christ Jesus for ever and ever. Amen. (Eph. 3,14-21).

Despite the scholarly debates about who actually wrote the letter to the Ephesians, I think that we can still say that St. Paul wants us to be filled with the utter fullness of God, because the whole letter is certainly "Pauline". This "utter fullness" is the contemplative value in Carmelite spirituality of which we speak a great deal. To be filled with the utter fullness of God is to be a mystic. Mysticism is not for an elite few; it is for everyone. It means to become an intimate friend of God. This is the call which we receive in baptism and mysticism or contemplation is the full flowering of the baptismal grace.

At present there is a thirst for God among people. Despite the present aggressive secularism, this thirst has not been dampened, though it does tend to be expressed in ways outside the Church. Those who profess a Christian faith often express this thirst in terms of prayer. Many people are seeking depth and a whole host of prayer groups have sprung up to answer this need. Carmelite

Carmel: The Future

spirituality can lead people to the source of living water where their thirst can be quenched. I see in the future much more concentration on the contemplative charism of Carmel. Those who are called to Carmel are called above all to be contemplatives. Let us be clear that a contemplative is not one who is enclosed in a monastery or a convent. There are contemplatives in every neighbourhood and in every area of life. One famous contemplative was Dag Hammarskjold who was Secretary General of the United Nations and obviously an extremely busy man. No-one of course knew that he was a mystic, nor I am sure did he. It was only after his death that his diary was discovered. The jottings there showed quite clearly that he was indeed a man of God. His diary has been published under the title of "Markings".[1] Mostly contemplatives do not know that they are such. Contemplation and mysticism really have the same meaning and I use the terms interchangeably. Being a contemplative or a mystic has nothing to do with visions or hearing voices or anything of that sort. Mystics can be the busiest people but in the midst of all their activity are seeking the One who is.

Mystics allow God to take flesh once again in their lives. People who follow this path become their true selves. We are called to follow Christ and to imitate him. Jesus was truly human because he was divine. We are not yet fully human; we are on the way. We become fully human when God unites us with Himself and we become like Him. Purgatory means that death is not the end of our journey; we have the opportunity to grow after death so that we can become what God knows we can be. We believe that we can help each other by our prayer and we can help those who have died to continue their journey through our prayer for them.

I believe that in the future there will be a much greater concentration on the path which leads to the fulfilment of all our yearnings. If we accept that we are called to be filled with the utter fullness of God, how do we arrive at that? The Carmelite way will come into its own because it is about leading and guiding people to the summit of Mount Carmel where God is all in all. This is never to be thought of as an individual venture. We need one another as we journey and the acid test of how we relate to God is always how we relate to one another. However there is a major problem in that we cannot arrive at our goal. This is impossible for us but not for God for nothing is impossible for God. (cf. Lk. 1, 38)

The emotional programmes

God desires to accomplish His will in us but He wants our co-operation. God will not force Himself on us. We must allow Him to dismantle our emotional programmes, so laboriously set up, that we mistakenly thought would bring us happiness so that He can invade our whole being and unite us with Himself. These emotional programmes are the major blocks within us to God's accomplishing His will in us. So what are these emotional programmes within us? These are ways by means of which we attempt to control our own lives and destiny.

What God desires to do in us is recreate us in the image of His Son. This is the true self which needs to emerge from the cocoon of the old self. From our earliest days we learn how to cope with the world and with people. We protect ourselves from perceived danger and we seek happiness. We gradually build up these emotional programmes for our own protection and happiness. Deep within us there is an instinct for survival which is healthy and good. It stops us from doing silly things and putting ourselves into obvious danger but it also drives us to seek security in many subtle ways. We tend to believe in God while trying to hold on to whatever it is that we think will make us feel secure. We can tell God that we trust in Him alone but the reality can be very different.

Also we need to be loved and we seek this love for our own well-being. However this deep human need and desire can easily be twisted. We can base our sense of self-worth on the level of love or affection which others have for us. Therefore we will manipulate people into gratifying our own needs and desires. However we are good and worthwhile simply because God has created us and loves us. Whatever people may think about us, that truth remains. So we must gradually let go of our clinging to people for the gratification of our need for affection. I am not and can never be defined by what people think of me. I can find the reflection of myself only in God.

The world can be perceived as a very threatening place and in order to feel secure we need to feel in control. Therefore there can be a tendency to seek power over things and people in order to maintain our control.

These three emotional centres as they are called - survival, affection and power are in each of us to a certain extent. We may tend towards one more strongly than another at times or even permanently. They do affect us in very subtle ways. The way to recognise when they are operating is through our emotions. Our instinctive reaction is to blame other people for our emotions – "You have hurt me" or "you have made me angry" or "it's all your fault". Of course you are not to blame for my feelings. They are my problem, not yours. The three emotional centres form the false self and it will defend itself by all means in its power. If you do not back up my opinion of myself by your attitude, I will strike out at you in some way - perhaps by anger or withholding my affection. If only the world, or my bosses or the organisation to which I belong were better then everything would be fine. But, I'm afraid, everything would not be fine. In the Gospel, Jesus challenges me personally to let go of the false self-system, to die to self so that the true self can be born. The one who holds onto his life will lose it; the one who loses his life for my sake and for the sake of the Gospel will save it. (cf. Mk 8,35)[2]

The challenge at the beginning of the Gospel is to repent and believe the Gospel which means turn around in your road and seek your happiness in God and in nothing else. An idol is any person, place or thing from which we look for the happiness that can come only from God. Our emotions and feelings faithfully record what our true values are even though we may think they are Gospel values. Therefore our emotions, not our words and concepts, will let us know whether in fact we are placing our trust in an idol or in the Living God

Taking this path involves us in a struggle which requires great honesty. This is the real penance. St. Thérèse of Lisieux, when she was preparing to enter Carmel, decided to live a life of mortification. She makes it clear that she does not mean that she took on physical penances. Instead she would do little things to thwart her own will, to hold back the cutting word and so on.[3] God calls us to freedom but freedom is not easy to come to. We have habitual ways of acting and responding from childhood and these ways are so ingrained in us that they are very difficult to eradicate. In the Sermon on the Mount, Jesus says, "*If someone strikes you on the right cheek, offer the other one too*". (Mt. 5, 39). This is not a pacifist manifesto but an invitation to freedom. Our habitual tendency is to strike back in some way when attacked. This is not just a physical thing. If you hurt me in some way, then I will seek, albeit in a subtle way, to repay you in kind. Jesus calls us to the freedom of not having to respond in this habitual way. We are called to unconditional acceptance and love of all people. Only God can do this and so only God can give us the freedom to act in this way also.

The false self system, based on the emotional programmes for happiness, can adapt itself to any kind of life style. It is just as effective in the spiritual life as it is in our exterior life. God must teach us that we cannot grasp hold of Him, nor can we control or manipulate Him. Of course we do not think that we are trying to do that, which is why our attachment to our emotional programmes for happiness is so subtle. We can cling onto feelings and consolations in prayer because they can give us a sense of getting somewhere in the spiritual life and in our relationship with God. Sometimes God will take these away so that we will learn by experience that only He, and not any of His gifts, no matter how sublime, can satisfy us.

Continuing on the inner journey will involve us in a long process whereby God reshapes us according to the image of His Son. The breaking down of the old self is painful but the birth of the new self makes all the pain worthwhile. Another term for this process is purification. We are purified so that we can receive God.

As we become more and more conscious of God's presence and action within us as the true source of all our happiness, we become more ready to dismantle the false self which we now perceive to be a burden. In the false self we have placed our hope for happiness and now slowly there develops within us a progressive self-forgetfulness and self-abandonment, confident in the power of God to lead us to the fullness of life. Our various likes, dislikes and desires gradually become a radical surrender to God's will not just at the time of prayer but also in daily life. In this way we become what God knows we can be.

Our spiritual heritage

In the future I see a greater concentration on the spiritual journey in the Church at large and in Carmel. We will become more and more aware of our spiritual heritage and how the insights of Carmelites who have gone before us can help us on our own journey and also help us to help others. Our spiritual tradition is very rich but it is little known. Many people associate Carmel with St. John of the Cross and think that it is only for a spiritual elite. We know that it speaks to us of the whole spiritual journey and gives all of us hope that we might, like Elijah, receive the food and drink necessary in order to journey to Horeb, the mountain of God. (cf. I Kings 19, 5-8). Carmelite spirituality is for people on a journey, the spiritual journey, moving towards God. It does not matter where the individual starts as long as he or she has a desire to journey towards God, then Carmelite spirituality can be of assistance.

I see in the future a continual flourishing of different lay movements within the Carmelite family. Just as the friars do not have a monopoly on the Carmelite charism, neither does the Third Order have a monopoly on how lay Carmelites can be a part of the Carmelite family. The Third Order is a particular way in which lay people can be members of the family. It may suit some people but not others. The Rule of St. Albert has proved over many centuries that it is a source of spiritual fruitfulness. Who knows what might emerge in the future?

How will the Third Order evolve in the future? That is lost in the mystery of God but perhaps I could share with you some ideas which I have. First of all I would see that the present Rule of the Third Order being expanded to become a commentary on the Rule of St. Albert suitable for lay people. The Rule of St. Albert is deceptively simple. It was originally written for hermits and then adapted for conditions in the West and for those who wished to commit themselves to an active apostolate while maintaining a focus on prayer and contemplation. There are many ways to read a text. One way is to ask what Albert meant when he wrote it and what the hermits understood by it. However this interpretation would not mean a great deal today. Another possible way of reading the text is to bring our own issues, concerns, questions and experiences and ask what the Rule has to say to us. We use this method of interpretation unconsciously when we read Scripture e.g. when we apply some of the Song of Songs to Our Lady. The writer of that Old Testament text did not have Our Lady in mind when he wrote but because of our Christian experience, we can see meanings in the text which go beyond what the original writer intended. Therefore let us read and reread the Rule of St. Albert as a gift from God to us, not as a "sacred text" which has an unchanging meaning but as a source of inspiration as to how we can adapt the

Carmel: The Future

original Carmelite inspiration to our changing needs and cultures.

The Rule is imbued with the Word of God. Short though it is, it contains about a hundred explicit or implicit Scriptural texts. The hermits were enjoined to ponder on the law of the Lord day and night. This pondering was intended to transform the individual into Christ from the inside out. We are to allow the Word of God to envelop us so that whatever we do will *"have the Lord's Word for accompaniment"* (ch.14). The same process of transformation is at work in all of us whatever our particular style of life. The Rule of St. Albert has inspired many different kinds of ways of life; it can also inspire members of the Third Order to live more deeply their Carmelite vocation at the heart of the world and its concerns.

The two inspirational models which Carmel presents to us, Mary and Elijah, are biblical figures who pondered long on the Word of God and gave it their whole-hearted assent. Carmel itself is imbued with the Word of God. I would see in the future far greater emphasis on lectio divina which can be translated as sacred reading. This is a way of pondering on the Scriptures and the model is the bee which is out to collect pollen. It does not just fly over many flowers; it has to enter inside and collect all the pollen before it flies on to another flower. This sacred reading can be done alone and also with a group. I would then see that the meetings of Carmelites would be very much concentrated on this sacred reading of Scripture. The members could be asked to bring their bibles which will probably be falling apart from constant use (!) and read a selected portion of Scripture together. This would be followed by silence for 10 to 15 minutes during which the members would simply listen to God in the depths of their own hearts. Then the group would share together what the particular Scriptural text means for each person. This would not be a discussion but a sharing of faith. The head is not the most important aspect of the reading but the heart. Lectio divina is a particular form of prayer but much more importantly it is the structure of all authentic Christian prayer and shapes the day with its flowing of reading, reflection, responding and resting. Following on from this greater emphasis on Holy Scripture, I would see the use of the Divine Office become the norm instead of the little office. The Divine Office is the Prayer of the whole Church and it is fitting for lay Carmelites to use this form of prayer.

I believe that there will be much greater emphasis on the Third Order as a lay organisation with elected national officials who will animate the local chapters with help from the friars when requested. Being a member of the Third Order is just as much a vocation as being a friar. The friars are not the sole custodians of the Carmelite charism. It is too rich and too multi-faceted for that. The Third Order will take its own direction and the friars will be advisers. More lay Carmelites will enter into ministries helping people to pray and to deepen their spiritual life. Perhaps for this the friars will be able to help by giving training and so on in the tradition. Unfortunately Carmelite spirituality is not quite as easily packaged as Ignatian spirituality. However perhaps this training will only come when there is a real demand for it.

We are being invited into God's future but what this will be like depends very much on our co-operation. How do you want to live out your Carmelite vocation? If you are perfectly happy with things as they are and want no change, then no change will take place because it is your vocation. Self-satisfaction is always a little dangerous. If however there is to be change it will mostly come from lay Carmelites themselves. Lay Carmelites must make known what they are looking for and how the Order as a whole can help.

I have only sketched in outline form some of the possibilities for the future. Each of these points could be developed much more. However perhaps you can develop them in your own time. We have been called together into the land of Carmel. Under the patronage of Our Lady and inspired by the prophet Elijah, may we co-operate with God as He helps us to grow both individually and as a family so that we all become what God knows we can be.

Endnotes

1 DAG HAMMARSKJÖLD, *Markings*, (Faber and Faber, London & Boston, 1964).
2 For a simple explanation of the false self and the emotional programmes that make it up, see ELIZABETH SMITH and JOSEPH CHALMERS, *A Deeper Love. An Introduction to Centering Prayer* (Continuum, London & New York, 1999).

3 A, 68v. This is a reference to the first manuscript of St. Thérèse's Autobiography or Story of a Soul, which was written when she was in the Carmel of Lisieux. It was written at the command of the then prioress, her sister Mother Agnes of Jesus (Pauline). There are so many published versions of this book that references are now normally given to the original French text." Throughout the book, references to Thérèse's autobiography is to manuscript A, B or C followed by the page in the original where it may be found. The text used is: Thérèse de L'Enfant-Jésus et de la Sainte face, *Oeuvres complètes*, (*Textes et Dernières Paroles*), (Éditions du Cerf, 1992, Desclée de Brouwer).

CARMELITES AND THE FUTURE

Mt. 28, 18 – "Jesus came and said to them, "All authority in heaven and on earth has been given to me.
19 Go therefore and make disciples of all nations, baptizing them in the name of the Father and of the Son and of the Holy Spirit,
20 and teaching them to obey everything that I have commanded you. And remember, I am with you always, to the end of the age."

This text spells out our task in the present and the future. We, as members of the Church, are to carry on the mission of Christ. The end of our Rule points us towards the future. Like the innkeeper in the story of the Good Samaritan, we continue our work while keeping an eye on the horizon waiting for the Master's return.[1]

More and more people in our western societies no longer count themselves as Christians. In some societies I suspect that the number of non-Christians and those who are actively opposed to the Catholic Church is growing. More and more children are being brought up with no sense of God. In fact, God does not enter into the thought of a number of people and is being excluded from many areas of human life. Religion is slowly being relegated to the private sphere as a personal hobby so long as it does not interfere with anyone else.

Abortion is often presented now as a human right and those who are opposed are painted as enemies of women and of human progress.

Creative Fidelity

In the midst of our changing world, the primary challenge for us as individuals and as an Order is unchanging. We are called to be constantly faithful to the charism that God has given to us in trust for the Church and the world. Being faithful does not necessarily mean repeating what has gone before. Times change and so we must change our way of living and presenting the charism so that it can be an effective vehicle of evangelisation in a new era. We do not of course change the charism but we can and do change the way it is presented; we also add to it and enrich it by how we live it in our own day. We can learn a great deal from the prophet Elijah in this connection.

God speaks to us in many ways. One of these ways is through the cultural changes that our world is undergoing at present. We cannot claim to be faithful to God if we do not ponder the Scriptures but equally we cannot claim to be faithful if we do not listen to what God is saying to us from the heart of the world. A new kind of evangelisation is required for a new situation. We must seek to understand what is going on and why and then respond the best way we can. Perhaps we hide the face of Christ from some people by our tired words and tired ways. We must be careful lest we find ourselves speaking in a language of yesterday to the people of tomorrow.

All consecrated men and women *"must continue to be images of Christ the Lord, fostering through prayer a profound communion of mind with him (cf. Phil 2, 5-11), so that their whole lives may be penetrated by an apostolic spirit and their apostolic work with contemplation."*[2] There can be no doubt that in the eyes of most people Carmel stands for prayer, contemplation, and the interior life. Carmelites do many different things, and that is one of our strengths, but in all these different apostolic works we are expected to express our spirituality. What we do must spring from what we are. We are most faithful to God when we are faithful to the vocation that has been given us. There is a distinction that I have always found helpful between working for God and doing God's work. We work for God in all sorts of ways and our apostolic labours may be very laudable but are they all according to the mind and heart of God? To do God's work means to do what God really wants of us. Our charism is spelled out clearly in our official documents. How do I incarnate this Carmelite vocation of living in allegiance to Jesus Christ through prayer, service and fraternity according to the inspiration of Our Lady and the Prophet Elijah?

The fundamental thrust of our lives has to do with the contemplative aspect of our charism. This does not mean that we all must become hermits but that we must be contemplatives in the midst of the different activities in which we are involved.

Our prophetic and apostolic activity will naturally flow from our contemplative life. We cannot be contemplatives if we do not spend time alone with God but more than that, it is a process whereby God purifies and transforms our hearts so that we become like God. This process requires our consent to the action of God in our lives and a recognition that God works often in very human ways. The whole thrust of our spiritual tradition is about this process in which God transforms our selfishness into pure love. God will use all the ordinary events of daily life to reveal to us who and what we are. This is a very painful process and therefore it is much easier to forget about prayer and immerse ourselves in working for God while perhaps forgetting to do God's work. Am I faithful but also creative? Are we, the Carmelite family, faithful to God and yet creative, so that we can proclaim the Good news in a way that people in our own culture can actually hear it?

Vocations

Despite the best efforts of vocation promoters, it seems that new vocations will be very few, at least for the foreseeable future, especially in the West. This will have major implications for the Church, the Order and each Province. To face up to closing houses or withdrawing from certain apostolic commitments can be very painful. However it is absolutely essential to prune the branches so that others may grow. If we do not close communities when necessary, it will mean that the men will suffer because they will have to do more and more work to cover what was done by more people in the past. Community life will also suffer. So, am I willing to let go of my apostolate and my house if the discernment of the brothers goes in that direction?

If our prayer is authentic, if it is a personal encounter with the One whom we know loves us, it will transform us from those who work for God into those who do God's work. We will begin to see people and situations no longer merely with our limited human sight but through the eyes of God. Our judgements will no longer be so conditioned by selfish considerations but our minds and hearts will be informed by the will of God. This will transform our way of being in the world. We will realise that we must plant or water the garden but only God can grant the growth.

Formation

Formation lasts at least a lifetime; we are not finished with it when we are solemnly professed. We have very good Constitutions and formation document. We have many more Carmelite resources available to us than in the past. Great progress has been made in the area of research and publishing. However, do we take the opportunities presented to us to read and reflect on this material so that we can deepen our understanding of the vocation to which we have been called?

What is formation for? It is an important ongoing process of growth. There is a need for continual Carmelite formation but we cannot be good Carmelites if we are not good human beings. There are certain basic human skills, which are required to make life in society bearable. If these have not been learned in the home environment, they must be quickly instilled at the beginning of formation. What happens when these ordinary human virtues are not learned during initial formation? Each of us has to ask ourselves whether we make community life pleasant or unpleasant for the others? There are several elements that must be borne in mind in the formation process. There is the human level, the intellectual level and the spiritual level. These elements obviously influence one another. All of these must be worked upon throughout the whole of life. These three elements are like the three legs of a stool. If one is out of balance, the whole stool is unbalanced. What about our lives? If there is an imbalance somewhere in our lives, what are we going to do about it? Formation is to help us in our becoming mature human beings, mature followers of Christ and mature Carmelites.

No one of course is perfect but hopefully all of us are on the spiritual journey. This journey requires a great deal from us because we are called to pass through the desert where we are purified and we grow to maturity in Christ. It is a great temptation to give up the journey because it is too difficult and settle down to mediocrity. In the post-synodal document Vita Consecrata, Pope John Paul II pointed out the importance of the various phases of the formation process. He writes of the middle years that this phase can present the risk of routine and the subsequent temptation to give in to disappointment because of meagre results.[3]

In this document it is also said, *"Those in charge of formation must therefore be very familiar with the path of seeking God, so as to be able to accompany others on this journey."*[4] Those who know something of the path of seeking God, know that there are moments of disappointment and disillusionment, times perhaps when we feel like the Prophet Elijah who sat under a bush and had no desire to continue. (I Kings 19, 4) It is vitally important, I believe, that in the process of formation, which lasts the whole of one's Carmelite life, we should be helped to first of all be aware that darkness, disillusionment and disappointment are normal stages on the journey.

We have a profound impact on those who come to us, even if they decide not to continue walking the same path as we walk and so we have a sacred duty to give our candidates the best formation we can possibly give them. What must we do to be continually faithful to this duty? We also have a great impact on those we serve in our apostolic activities. What kind of impact do we have?

Carmelite Family

The Carmelite Family has grown and developed greatly in recent years with many new members and new groups. New ways of understanding the relationships between the different components within the Family are emerging.

Despite the decline in religious observance, it has often been said that there is a great thirst for spirituality around the world. This takes many paths but certainly many people seem to be fascinated by the Carmelite way. This puts a lot of pressure on us. It is not sufficient to be a good parish priest or a good physics teacher but the people expect us to know something of the spiritual journey, not only theoretically but also from our own experience. Lay people are becoming more knowledgeable about Carmelite spirituality and some desire to live it in new ways. All of this puts pressure on the friars and perhaps disturbs our comfortable life. What is our reaction to lay Carmelites? Can we see the hand of God present in some way through them?

Justice and peace

As a contemplative fraternity at the service of God's people, we take to heart the words of Vita Consecrata that the Christ encountered in contemplation is the same who lives and suffers in the poor.[5] The same number speaks of the option for the poor as being inherent in the very structure of love lived in Christ.

> *All of Christ's disciples are held to this option, but those who wish to follow the Lord more closely, imitating his attitudes, cannot but feel involved in a very special way. The sincerity*

> *of their response to Christ's love will lead them to live a life of poverty and to embrace the cause of the poor.*

The Provinces and Commissariats of the Order have been very generous in their support of many projects. However each one of us has to look at his or her life before God and ask whether he/she sees Christ in the poor as well as in prayer.

Mission

> *"Those who love God, the Father of all, cannot fail to love their fellow human beings, whom they recognise as brothers and sisters. Precisely for this reason, they cannot remain indifferent to the fact that many men and women do not know the full manifestation of God's love in Christ. The result, in obedience to Christ's commandment, is the missionary drive ad gentes."*[6]

The Order has always had a missionary thrust and Carmelites have preached the Gospel and planted the Order in many new lands. However, clearly a change is developing in the Church and the Order. There are far fewer young men coming forward in the older Provinces while there are many in the developing nations. How are we going to handle this changing reality? How is the Order going to continue to be missionary with far fewer vocations? How is each one of us going to carry out our task of teaching others to obey everything that Christ has taught us? We teach first of all by the example of our lives. What do our lives say to people?

Conclusion

When I look towards the future, I am full of hope. The Order will surely be different but, as Cardinal Newman said, *"To live is to change, and to be perfect is to have changed often"*[7]. Our task is to be faithful to our vocation and to try to read the signs of the times, i.e. to discern what God is saying to us from the heart of the world. We can only do that effectively if we have a contemplative heart.

Endnotes

1. This idea comes from KEES WAAIJMAN, *The Mystical Space of Carmel. A Commentary on the Carmelite Rule* (Peeters, Fiery Arrow series, 1999), p. 250-255.
2. Vita Consecrata, 9.
3. Vita Consacrata 70.
4. Ibid., 66.
5. Ibid., 82.
6. Ibid., 77.
7. Cf. JOHN HENRY NEWMAN, *An Essay on the Development of Christian Doctrine* (1845). This has been republished in many editions and no doubt there will be many future editions as Newman's beatification draws near.

CARMEL AND HOPE

We live in a beautiful world but at the same time it is wracked with problems. Every day we are faced with awful news – rampant poverty, our world being destroyed by consumerism and climate change, political corruption in many countries, trafficking in human beings, child abduction, murder and of course terrorism. In many countries the Church has suffered tremendously with a number of cases of clerical sexual abuse. These have brought shame on the whole Church and priests and religious especially feel this shame. There are also problems in community living and in our apostolates. Perhaps community life or the Order are not what we thought when we joined. They do not always respond to our hopes. Perhaps we believe that the Church is going the wrong way. However in the midst of all these depressing problems, we are bearers of a profound hope that comes from our spirituality. We are being invited into the Kingdom of God but in order to enter, we must change. We are on a journey of transformation.

We Carmelites, like all Christians, are called to live in allegiance to Jesus Christ. The first Carmelites went to live in the land of the Lord, where Jesus lived, died and rose again. They were very aware that they were following in the footsteps of the crucified Christ. Yes, he is the risen glorified Lord but he first was crucified. So death and darkness are an important part of the Christian life. They do not have the last word but they nevertheless exist.

As we know, the heart of the Carmelite charism is contemplation, which is a process of purification and transformation by means of which we grow in our relationship with God so that we will see with God's eyes and love with God's heart. We are invited onto a journey of transformation that brings us into the mystery of God. This is the basis for our hope despite, and perhaps because of all that is happening around us.

Going on a Journey

The theme of journey is very important in our spirituality. The Ratio, the fundamental formation document for the friars, takes up this theme to describe the movement towards transformation. When you feel that problems are overwhelming, it is a good idea to remind yourself of what is the heart of our vocation and you can find this powerfully described in the first part of the Constitutions and in the Ratio.

The Ratio speaks of a journey, a process, of formation that does not end when we are solemnly professed or ordained. It goes on until our ultimate transformation whenever that may be. This life journey takes us through all sorts of experiences, ups and downs, highs and lows. Sometimes we get stuck in a ditch and need help to get out and continue our journey. It is difficult at times to accept that we need help. There are people who deny that they have a problem and blame everyone else for the state in which they find themselves. They do not want to face their demons and so they simply deny what is obvious to everyone around them. They can make the life of everyone else in the community very difficult. Often confrontation is avoided and we settle for dysfunctional lives and dysfunctional communities. In our days the Church is reaping the harvest of failure to confront problems in the past.

It can seem at times that there is no guiding principle except blind fate. Many people live their lives according to that belief in practice even though they may profess some form of religion. According to our faith, there is a movement and we are not just wandering around blindly going nowhere. For the journey towards transformation, faith is required. Faith is not just an intellectual adherence to revealed truth; it is a life option made each day often despite appearances that militate against faith. To continue the journey to the end we need to believe that God is very close to us, within us, around us, again often despite what we see and feel.

Into the Castle

According to the famous example, so brilliantly worked out in detail by St. Teresa of Avila, God lives at the centre of our being and the journey of faith is from the periphery of our life to the centre. We are indeed fortunate to have both Teresa and John of the Cross as members of our Family; they were formed in the Carmelite tradition, took the traditional elements and restated them in a profound way. Teresa describes the interior of the human being as a beautiful castle with many fascinating rooms. The most beautiful room is in the very centre where lives the King, i.e. God. Outside the castle is a rather dangerous place with all sorts of nasty reptiles. Many people live outside the castle and do not seem to be aware of their pitiful state. The way into the castle is prayer, understood as communication with God.[1] Some prayer does not appear to be communication with God at all. Sometimes it is simply talking to oneself or daydreaming. So we must seek a way of prayer that truly opens us to communicate with God. Lectio Divina brings us into contact with the Word of God and opens us to God's transforming presence and action. Lectio Divina enlivened Carmelite life for many centuries and has been rediscovered in our own days.

Once inside the castle, there are lots of rooms to explore. The first rooms we come across are those of self-knowledge. We must enter these rooms and continually return to them. The rooms of self-knowledge are important but they are not the end of the journey. Without self-knowledge we would not get very far on the journey. Teresa says humility is vital and in her understanding, humility means simply to know and accept the truth about oneself.[2] How difficult it is to know and accept the truth about ourselves! In our days we are offered all sorts of counselling and therapies; hopefully these help us to know ourselves and to use that knowledge as a basis for continued growth and not to stop at navel gazing. Growing in the relationship with God affects how we relate to other human beings. It is self-delusion to think that one is close to God when one does not even treat other people with simple human courtesy.

Most people reach the third mansions fairly quickly but Teresa points out a serious problem. Apparently many people reach this point and do not move on and the reason seems to be that they become self-satisfied and see no need for further effort.[3] The problem here is that it is a good state. Individuals who arrive at this point are good people but their religion is guided always by common sense; they are never tempted to go too far. However there is still a long way to go. The journey must continue.

The prophet's example

In order to continue the journey, we need a little push from time to time. Remember the scene where Elijah sits under a bush and wishes that he were dead. (I Kings 19, 4). God has a plan for him and the divine plan could be thwarted if Elijah does not continue his journey so God sends an angel. This divine messenger gives Elijah a push, offering food and drink. The angel has to repeat the process before Elijah is willing to get up and continue his journey. We have no facile answers to the problems of the world. It is an insult and a blasphemy to assure someone who is crushed by some event or illness that it is the will of God. Why bad things happen to good people or why bad things happen at all is a mystery. When Jesus was crucified, he experienced the absence of God and especially in our modern day, this is a very common experience. God seems to be absent from our modern world. Many people, even believers, seem to be practical atheists in the sense that they live as though God did not exist even though they might go to church on a Sunday.

Where is God in the midst of all our problems? Our faith tells us that God cannot really be absent from our lives. That would be hell. But perhaps we need to learn to discern the presence of God in the apparent absence of God and to learn a new language, God's language. Our brother, John of the Cross, tells us that,

> *One word the Father spoke,*
> *which word was His Son,*
> *and this word he speaks*
> *ever in eternal silence,*
> *and in silence must it*
> *be heard by the soul*[4]

We have to cultivate a profound silence within so that we can hear what God wants to say to us. We need to listen to God in prayer of course but also in the events of daily life. Often we have so much noise going on inside us that we cannot hear or discern anything else. As Carmelites, this silence should come naturally to us, or at least the desire for it. This is not just an ascetic practice and it is not referring merely to an external silence. It is an internal silence in order to discern the presence of God in the midst of even the most hopeless situation so that we can continue our journey with hope.

We need to try to identify the noise inside us: the commentaries on others, on events, and on ourselves. Once we have become aware of our internal noise, we can begin to let it go so that it does not influence everything we do, think and say. If we continue the journey we will be brought face to face with our prejudices, our irrational fears and our presumptions. This experience is not to depress us but so that we can be liberated from them.

It is necessary to cultivate an interior silence so that we will be aware that God is speaking to us through some simple and humble messenger. If we are not silent within, life passes us by and we never grasp the true significance of what happens to us. It is interesting to have a period of silence with a group. After a few seconds, the coughing starts, then the shifting in seats, the odd rustling of paper can be heard. Many of us are not completely at ease with external silence. We wake up in the morning and turn on the radio. We spend our day working where we are often surrounded by noise of all kinds; we do not have much time even to think. We have an internal tape or cd that comments on everything and everyone throughout the day. The comments on the internal tape are based on our particular perspective on life, which of course is usually in our favour. We instinctively defend ourselves if we feel under attack and we seek the esteem and acceptance of others. We do this usually without being aware of what is going on inside us. It is a constant internal noise that makes it difficult to hear any other voice. The journey of faith towards transformation takes us through bright sunlight and dark valleys. God uses all the events of our life, good and bad, as instruments of purification, which is essential if we are to become what God has created us to be. We have to make the effort to attempt to discern the hand of God at work but this discernment is much easier if we can calm the noise inside us and hear the voice of God who speaks in the sound of the gentle breeze, or as some exegetes have it, "*the sound of sheer silence*" (I Kings 19, 13).

Remember the experience of Elijah. He has just won a great victory for Yahweh on Mount Carmel but he is threatened by Jezebel and immediately his internal noise drowns out his trust in God. He goes into the desert, which is traditionally the place of silence. God speaks to Elijah through the angel so that Elijah will continue his journey. Elijah has difficulty in discerning the voice of God in the midst of all his troubles but eventually plods on to Horeb. When he arrives there, God asks him what he is doing there. Elijah replies that he is filled with great zeal for the Lord God of hosts. He tells God that he is the only champion of Yahweh remaining in the whole of Israel. God does not respond at this point but simply tells Elijah to go out and stand on the mountain. There Elijah meets God but not in the way he expects nor in the way that his whole religious tradition has taught him to expect. Elijah has to silence all his internal voices that tell him what God is like so that he can receive God as God is. Once Elijah has met God on God's terms, and not on his own terms, he is open to hear the truth, which sets him free from illusion. He thought that God really needed him since he was the only prophet left. God very gently points out that in fact there are 7000 others who have not bent the knee to Baal. Now freed from illusion, Elijah receives a new mission from God, which is in fact mostly carried out by his successor, Elisha, who is the recipient of a double portion of his spirit.[5]

Into the desert

In our faith journey, there are moments when we as individuals or as groups are brought into the desert. Sometimes we walk into the desert following God's call or sometimes we just find ourselves there by force of circumstance. The desert is arid and it can be a frightening place. What does it all mean? We have tried our best to be faithful to Christ's call to follow him. We have worked in Carmelite parishes or schools for a number of years and for a variety of reasons, the future looks bleak. As priests and religious, we have lost status and we can be tempted not to go any further on the journey because we feel it is just not worth all the trouble. Then God sends a messenger to us. This messenger can come in all shapes and sizes and he or she encourages us to eat and drink for the journey is long. We are encouraged to eat the bread of life and drink from Carmel's wells, that is the Carmelite tradition, which has given life to many generations before us and is responsible for new life springing up all over the world. But perhaps we are too depressed to even be aware of this, so God's messenger nudges us again and encourages us to eat and drink. It is a great challenge to recognise what God is saying to us in the midst of daily life and to recognise the voice of God in and through the voice of some very unlikely person.

I do not know whether God causes everything that happens to us but I believe firmly that God is in the midst of every event, good or bad. God uses everything, big or small, good or bad, to challenge our normal way of being in the world, just as Elijah was challenged to let go of his expectations of how God would come to him. These expectations were deeply rooted in Elijah and our expectations and perspectives are deeply implanted in us. Before we can receive God as God really is, we have to learn to let go of all these. This is a painful process, a real dark night, but essential so that we can bear the light of day and be prepared for the encounter with God.

Our Carmelite tradition speaks of a journey of transformation. The events of our life are not meaningless. At the heart of every event, God is calling to us to take a step forward on our journey. God is calling to us to take a step forward from our predictable way of judging people, including ourselves, and situations to begin to see things from God's perspective. The end of our journey is our transformation when we are able to look upon all that is as if with God's eyes and love what we see as if with God's heart. We need to eat and drink lest the journey be too long for us. We find the necessary food for our journey in the daily celebration of the Eucharist, pondering the Word of God and in our Carmelite tradition.

Our faith, hope and love, those three essential Christian virtues, are at the beginning of our journey, based on what we have learned from others. As we continue on the journey, our human reasons for belief, for hoping in God and for loving as Christ commanded, begin to fail us. They are no longer sufficient. We can throw it all in because the journey is too precarious and the end is uncertain or we can reject the messenger and stay right where we are. Or we can continue the journey into the night. An essential element on our journey towards transformation is the dark night. This was never intended to be gloomy and impossible but an invitation to let go of our human and limited way of thinking, loving and acting so that we can think, love and act according to God's ways.

John of the Cross gives masterful descriptions of various elements that go to make up the night but it is not uniform for everyone. The night is experienced by each person in a different way and is made precisely to assist the purification of the particular individual. The dark night is not a punishment for sin or infidelity but is a sign of the nearness of God. The dark night is God's work and leads to the complete liberation of the human person. For this reason it is to be welcomed despite the pain and confusion involved. The dark night can be experienced not only by individuals but by groups and whole societies.

The journey of transformation usually lasts a long time because the purification and change that is wrought in the human being is so profound. This is not just a change of idea or opinion; it is a complete transformation of how we relate to the world around us, to other people and to God. There is a saying about walking a mile in someone else's shoes before we can understand another person. Jesus warned his followers not to judge (Mt. 7, 1; Lk. 6, 37) and the reason is very simple: we cannot see things from another person's perspective and therefore we do not know what are the motives behind his or her actions. The process of Christian transformation, however, leads the human being towards a profound change of perspective, from his/her own particular way of seeing things to God's way. This involves a profound purification and emptying of all our attachments so that we can be filled with God.

Of course we need to make plans and goals and work towards their realisation. All of this needs to be done in an atmosphere of prayer in order to attempt to discern God's will and not just do what the majority wants, or even worse, to do what we want as individuals in a selfish way. No matter how much time we spend praying about our plans before we make decisions, there is no guarantee of their success. We know by bitter experience that all sorts of problems can arise to spoil our plans and to thwart our intentions.

This experience must not make us fatalists, refusing to plan ahead for fear of failure. We are called to work with Jesus Christ for the development of God's Kingdom. In order to become citizens of the Kingdom of God, we must change. God is creating a masterpiece in the life of each one of us and is bringing about the fulfilment of His plan of salvation through our lives and through our work. The great artist usually does not like to display an unfinished work and so we are not permitted to see what God is doing before the time. God is at work in our world and in our lives. Let us try to co-operate with God by continuing the journey towards transformation. Our Lady accompanies us on this journey as our Mother, Sister and Patroness. So do not let us falter. *"Eye has not seen nor has ear heard, nor has the human heart conceived what God has in store for those who love him."* (1 Cor. 2,9).

Endnotes

1   *Interior Castle*, 1, 7.
2   *Life*, 10, 4.
3   *Interior Castle,* III, 1, 2.
4   This quote is from the translation of E. Allison Peers, *The Complete Works of St. John of the Cross,* (Anthony Clarke, Wheathampstead, Hertfordshire, republished in 1974). It is cited as *Points of Love, 21.* In the more modern translation, Kieran Kavanaugh and Otilio Rodriguez, T*he Collected Works of St. John of the Cross* (ICS Publications,

Institute of Carmelite Studies, Washington D.C., 1979), the same saying is cited as *Maxims and Counsels*, 21.
5. For a development of the stories concerning the Prophet Elijah from a prayer perspective, see, JOSEPH CHALMERS, T*he Sound of Silence, Listening to the Word of God with Elijah the Prophe*t, (St. Albert's Press & Edizioni Carmelitane, Faversham & Rome, 2007).

CARMELITE PRAYER: SOURCE OF ENERGY

Pope John Paul II wrote an important letter at the close of the great jubilee of the year 2000 entitled *Novo Millennio Ineunte*. In this letter he invited all Christian communities to become "schools of prayer". He understood that the point of Christian teaching is to be a training in holiness and he went on to write:

> *This training in holiness calls for a Christian life distinguished above all in the art of prayer... Prayer develops that conversation with Christ which makes us his intimate friends: 'Abide in me and I in you' (Jn.15,4). This reciprocity is the very substance and soul of the Christian life... Wrought in us by the Holy Spirit, this reciprocity opens us, through Christ and in Christ, to contemplation of the Father's face. Learning this Trinitarian shape of Christian prayer and living it fully, above all in the liturgy, the summit and source of the Church's life, but also in personal experience, is the secret of a truly vital Christianity, which has no reason to fear the future, because it returns continually to the sources and finds in them new life. (art. 32)*

The Carmelite Family has sought from the very beginning to be "a school for prayer". The first hermits on Mt. Carmel, what were they seeking? They left nothing in writing unfortunately but we do know their fundamental ideas because St.

Albert of Jerusalem based himself on the proposal of the hermits when he wrote the original document 800 years ago that was finally approved as the Carmelite Rule in 1247. The values in the Rule of St. Albert, rooted in Scripture, are the foundation of all Carmelite life. The Carmelite saints have expanded on these throughout the succeeding centuries. The early Carmelites sought to live in allegiance to Jesus Christ; a concept that has at its centre the following of Christ but also includes a close family relationship with him. The hermits took as models for their following of Christ, Our Lady and the Prophet Elijah. The Prophet Elijah was the model for all early monks and hermits. Living on Mount Carmel, the first Carmelites could not have failed to be aware of his example. Throughout the centuries the Carmelites focused on Elijah as a great contemplative, who heard the voice of God in the sound of a gentle breeze or in the sound of sheer silence. With regard to Our Lady, the early Carmelites focused on the mysteries of her life that show her closeness to God. One of the Carmelite favourites was the mystery of Mary's motherhood, which they understood as a symbol of her intimacy with God. The hermits looked to Mary and Elijah to lead them on this journey into intimacy with the Lord.

So Carmelites have always sought intimacy with God. Those first men, who left their own countries to live in allegiance to Christ in his own land, took up the spiritual armour and weapons instead of those used in the very real war being waged very close to them. They wanted to live as hermits and yet together in community. They sought God in the silence of their individual cells and also together at Mass and when they shared meals. When these men left Mount Carmel and began to settle in the new cities that were springing up, they took the silence of the holy mountain with them in their hearts. They lived the same fundamental vocation but in a different way and in a different setting. Their experience is the beginning of the worldwide Carmelite Family - women and men who live the same values in different ways and in different ages, always seeking to live in allegiance to Jesus Christ wherever they find themselves.

Growing in friendship

Prayer is an essential part of the Carmelite charism. We are expected to be people of prayer and to form prayerful communities. Prayer is certainly what Carmel stands for in the minds of most people throughout the world.

The heart of the Carmelite way is contemplation. This does not refer to visions and other such phenomena but to an intimate relationship with God. All Carmelites, and especially our saints, have followed this path of growing in friendship with God in Jesus Christ until they can see as God sees and love as God loves. When we speak of "Carmelite Prayer", we are not referring to any specific method but to the way that Carmelites have prayed over the centuries and how they have written about prayer.[1]

The formation document of the friars, the Ratio (art. 29) makes a distinction between prayer and contemplation, while saying that in the Carmelite tradition prayer has often been identified with contemplation. Prayer is the door to contemplation.[2] In the Rule we have a balance between prayer in common and time alone with God in the cell. Certainly liturgical prayer is the highest form of prayer since it is the prayer of Christ directed towards the Father in the Holy Spirit. When we celebrate liturgy we are sharing in this prayer, in this intimate communication between the Father and the Son, which is the Holy Spirit.

For the Carmelite, the daily celebration of the liturgy is very important. Consecrated religious are deputed to celebrate the divine office in the name of the Church for the world. This is a very serious commitment, which we accept at solemn profession. Very many lay Carmelites throughout the world also pray the Divine Office daily. However celebrating liturgy in certain moments of the day does not suffice. The liturgy must affect every moment of our life. That is the idea of the Liturgy of the Hours, to sanctify the whole day and to bring to mind the presence of God at each moment. It is also very important not only to celebrate but to live the Eucharist, to learn from the example of Christ how to give ourselves to others, to live in the presence of God. Therefore the Eucharist and the Liturgy of the Hours are not momentary celebrations but are the heart of each day. It is from the liturgy that we gain the strength to serve the People of God and to live in harmony with others.

Methods of prayer

The Carmelite tradition makes one or two suggestions regarding methods of prayer suitable for people who are eager to respond to the grace of God. The aim of all Carmelite prayer is increasing friendship with God in Jesus Christ, which leads to the transformation of oneself so that we see as God sees and love as God loves. To aid this increasing friendship, the Carmelite tradition suggests keeping the relationship alive by using frequent aspirations e.g. "Jesus", "My Lord and My God" etc. However the Carmelite tradition does not espouse any particular method of prayer but is a living tradition in which very many saints have been formed, both known and unknown. It is indeed a source of continual energy and a school for life. St. Teresa of Avila said that there were very many ways to pray[3] what was important was not to think much but to love much.[4] Let us continually seek to love God, listening for God's voice at the time of prayer and in the midst of daily life. God, who has called us, is always faithful. By means of this ancient Carmelite tradition, may we be drawn deeper and deeper into the life of God so that we will be able to see as God sees and to love as God loves.

The Practice of the Presence of God

It was the Discalced Carmelite Lawrence of the Resurrection who first lived and made famous the practice of the presence of God.[5] This practice is very simple and at the same time very difficult. The Rule reminds us: *"let all you do have the Lord's word for accompaniment"*. (Rule 19). This is an echo of the letter to the Colossians: *"Whatever you do, whether in speech or in action, do it in the name of the Lord Jesus"*. (Col. 3,17). The practice of the presence of God is a simple method of prayer because it does not require any complicated regulations. It means simply to live in the truth. God is present in each moment of our lives, keeping us in existence, and this practice involves sharing everything that happens with God. It is not necessary to talk to God only of holy things; we can talk to God about whatever concerns us and share with God whatever happens to us. Lawrence of the Resurrection talked to God about all the practical details of his work as the cook and community bursar. God is in the midst of the reality that surrounds us whatever that may be. We do not bring Christ into situations; he is already there before us.

The practice of the presence of God is a way of continuing the dialogue with God throughout the entire day. The Second Vatican Council stressed the danger of dividing faith and life.[6] They are one and they should be one. Sharing the events of the day is a way of allowing the Word of God to influence everything we do, think or say. If we are not ashamed to do or say something in the presence of God, either we are living an illusion or our actions and words really are according to the will of God. Our false self will of course bring up all kinds of reasons to assure us that we are right and that we do not need to change. In order to live in the presence of God and indeed to walk the spiritual path, honesty is a sometimes painful but nevertheless essential virtue.

Devotion to Mary, the Mother of Jesus

Marian devotion is intimately connected to the Carmelite Order in the minds of most people. Mary is the Patroness, Mother and Sister of Carmelites and each of us has to work out his or her own relationship with her. The rosary is an enduring popular devotion and of course there are innumerable ways of using it for prayer. It is only limited by the creativity of each person. The most important symbol of Marian devotion among Carmelites is of course the scapular. There have been a number of attempts to re-envision this symbol for our times. On the occasion of the 750th anniversary of the scapular devotion, the Pope wrote a letter to the Order in which he described its two fundamental elements.[7] The scapular is part of the whole ensemble of Carmelite spirituality and it specifically reminds us of the constant presence of Mary in our lives. She is the mother of the divine life within us and she accompanies us that it may grow within us until we become transformed in God, which is the goal of our existence. The second fundamental element of the scapular devotion is our commitment to put on the virtues of Mary. She is the one above all who listened to the Word of God.[8]

In the Gospel that we use for the Solemnity of Our Lady of Mount Carmel, we hear Jesus' words from the cross as he gave Mary to the beloved disciple as mother to son. Then the Evangelist tells us that the disciple took Mary "into his own". Often this is translated as" he took her into his home" but the Greek need not mean that. It might mean that the beloved disciple, representing all of us, took Mary into what was most precious to him. What characterises the beloved disciple above all is his relationship with Jesus. Therefore he took Mary into his relationship with Jesus and Mary took the disciple (us) into her own relationship with her Son.[9]

A time to be alone with God is essential if we are going to grow in our relationship with God and it is what gives life to our liturgical celebrations. There are various ways to pray but all of them are directed towards establishing an intimate friendship with Jesus Christ so we should not get too bogged down with externals but do whatever increases our love for the Lord. The only way to judge prayer is whether it changes our lives, that is are we treating other people just a little bit better? The Constitutions of the Order remind us that:

> *A life of prayer also requires us to examine our way of life in the light of the Gospel, so that prayer may influence both our personal lives and the lives of our communities (art. 81).*

The Word of God at the centre

Prayer is our response to God who first approaches us. When we pray, in some way we enter into a relationship with God.

Personal relationships take time, energy and a commitment in order to develop. We must find something in common with the other person. What we have in common with God is Jesus Christ. He is the culmination of all that God has done for the world, and in Christ can be found everything that God wants to say to humanity. In the Scriptures we read the story of how God spoke to the people and what God wants to say. The whole of Scripture leads us to the fullness of the revelation of God in Christ.

The rediscovery of the centrality of the Word of God in the Church, led to the rediscovery also of the ancient practice of Lectio Divina. This was the normal way of prayer of the ancient monks and from them passed on to all the older religious orders. Lectio Divina is not only a method of prayer, but is a way of life; it is not just yet another thing to be fitted in to our already overcrowded schedules, but rather is the element that shapes our whole day according to the will of God. It is in fact the form of all Christian prayer. According to an ancient tradition, there are four fundamental moments in this way of prayer, Reading, Meditation, Prayer and Contemplation, or to put these another way: Read, Reflect, Respond and Rest. These moments are not strictly separated but flow into each other naturally and other moments can be added. Prayer is a very personal thing and each person must follow where the Spirit leads. The four traditional moments of Lectio Divina are simply an indication of the basic elements that make up Christian prayer.

The Word of God was the heart and soul of Carmelite prayer from the very beginning. The structure of the hermits' day was based on moving deeper into the Word of God, not so that they would assimilate it but so that the Word would assimilate them and they would become Christ. Carmelite prayer uses Lectio Divina not just as a method but as the structure within which the whole relationship with God and with the world can develop. The four fundamental moments of the traditional way of Lectio Divina: reading the Word, reflecting on the Word, responding to the Word and resting in the Word are four traditional steps, from the Carmelite viewpoint, of growing in intimacy with the Lord. This growing intimacy is the true source of energy and a school for life.

Prayer is rather like soup. Good soup (prayer) has these four elements as basic ingredients, but each cook will have a different recipe. The soup will have a different taste according to the quantity of each ingredient and according to what other ingredients are added. We have a great freedom in our relationship with God but Lectio Divina contains the wisdom of centuries of living the Christian life. Lectio Divina is not a rigid method but changes according to the person who follows its rhythm.

Read

Lectio Divina is the structure in which every solid relationship with God grows. So the first step is to read the Word of God. We can do this in many ways. We listen to the Scriptures at Mass, read the psalms in the Divine Office; we repeat the words of Scripture when we recite the rosary. Fundamentally this step is focused on getting acquainted with God. How do we do that? Growing in relationship with God has some similarities with the way we grow in relationship with another human being. The "getting to know you" process is not always easy.

What to say to God? Fortunately God provides topics of conversation in the Scriptures. The important thing is to get to know God who is fully revealed in Jesus Christ. This is the first step and takes time and effort. Do not complain that you are unfit if you do not take the time to exercise. It takes commitment. Just so with prayer. It can be laborious at certain points of the journey and especially at the beginning. The first ingredient then is *Lectio* (the traditional name), or, in other words, a time to read the Word of God, which is possible in a great variety of ways. Looking at frescoes and stained glass windows was the way in which uneducated people in the middle ages could "read" the Scriptures. Of course these things can still speak very powerfully to us today. The same can be said for statues, tapestries and any way of telling the biblical stories. To read the Word of God with profit, we must listen attentively in order to receive what God wants to give us. Clearly it is not sufficient to listen to the Word; we must also put it into practice as Mary, the mother of Jesus, did. (cf. Lk. 11, 27-28).

The Word of God is the story of God's relationship with the human family; it is the story of my and your relationship with God. By means of the Word, God speaks personally to you and to me. God wants to say something particular to us, and if we do not listen, we will not receive this very important message. When we read the Scriptures, it is necessary to take time, lest the Word goes in one ear and out the other without touching our hearts.

At this stage of our life, we are willing to give some time to God. We are beginning to take God seriously and we give some time to God although we are still easily distracted from God. A comparable stage in human relationships might be dating. The possibility of marriage has never been mentioned; the couple is trying each other out. It is vital that each accept the other as he or she is.

Of course the human comparison only takes us so far. In the human-divine relationship there is a strong element of teaching. Look at the experience of the disciples. Jesus chooses them and calls them to follow him. We do not know exactly how this took place but these men followed him in response to a call. At first there was great success. Crowds followed Jesus everywhere and they were mightily impressed by his miracles. The first disciples became suddenly important as friends of the great man. Very early on in Jesus' ministry, he gives his disciples a very important lesson about discipleship. We have a picture of a busy day in the life of Jesus in the Gospel of Mark, chap 1. He spent all day teaching and healing in Capharnum. Peter's mother in law was healed from her fever. Imagine how the people felt. This great teacher and miracle worker was going to set up his base in their town. Peter was obviously the right hand man. When night fell, all went off to bed. Early the next morning, the people came back to Peter's house looking for another show but Jesus was nowhere to be found! Peter, his great friend, goes searching and eventually finds him. Jesus was in deep communion with his Father but Peter had no qualms about interrupting. *"Everyone is looking for you!"* What was the response of Jesus? He did not go back with Peter but he said, *"Let us move on to the neighbouring villages so that I may proclaim the Good News there also."* In this way he invited the disciples to follow him wherever he goes and not try to shape Jesus to their will. He offers a similar invitation to us.

Jesus focuses on the formation of his disciples and he very gradually brings them to faith in himself as the Son of God. He walks on water and invites Peter to come to him (Mk 6, 45-52; Mt. 14, 22-33; Jn. 6, 16-21). Peter finally professes his faith in Jesus. This scene is in all the synoptic Gospels but the clearest for our purposes is in Mt. 16, 13-28. *"Who do you say I am?"* Peter recognised that Jesus was the messiah but he could not accept how Jesus understood his mission and for this Jesus called him a "satan", or a stumbling block. What kind of faith do we have? Do we believe in a God that suits our little mindset or in God as God really is? On the way to Jerusalem the disciples can be found arguing about who is to be the greatest! (Mk. 9, 33-37; Mt. 18, 1-4; Lk. 9, 46-48). The Gospels stress the fragility of the apostles on whom the Church is built. Why? I believe that this is to encourage us and to show us how to grow in relationship with Christ avoiding certain pitfalls.

Towards the end of John's Gospel, Jesus at the last supper says that he does not call them disciples any more but friends because he has revealed to them everything he has learned from his Father. (Jn. 15, 15) The goal of this relationship is transformation in Christ. Carmelite spirituality focuses particularly on this transformation and stresses contemplation, which is an intimate knowing and being known. Contemplation is the process that leads towards transformation. Carmelite prayer assumes the first two stages of the relationship with God - making the acquaintance of God and getting to know God - and it focuses on the latter stages of the relationship - growing in friendship and moving into intimacy.

Reflect

The second moment or ingredient of Lectio Divina is *meditatio*. This term, which means meditation, is very wide and so it is necessary to define it a little. In our western European tradition, to meditate is equivalent to reflect on God or on the things of God. In Buddhism, on the contrary it seems to means rather: "not thinking", and includes the various techniques used to arrive at this. In the traditional idea of reflecting on God or on some point of our faith, we try to enter more profoundly into the mystery of God or the mysteries of the faith. For example, we can spend a little time thinking about the Eucharist, starting from a text of Scripture. Then we could think about what the Eucharist means for us today. We receive Christ as our food so that we might begin to live like him. This is only one example among many of a meditation. We have a brain and we must use it also in the area of our faith life.

There is another more ancient type of meditation. At the beginnings of Christianity, meditation involved the whole body. When the first Carmelite hermits lived on Mount Carmel in the early 13th century, they understood meditation as a method for affixing the words of Sacred Scripture, and especially the psalms, in the mind and heart. Every hermit repeated the scriptural words over and over, with special emphasis on the psalms, often in a loud voice. That is probably one reason their cells were originally quite far apart so that each would not be disturbed by the noise of the other. Gradually it was hoped that the Word of God would transform their hearts.

Meditation, then, can have for us today also these different meanings: to reflect on the Word of God in order to apply it to one's own life, or repeat the words slowly in order to fix them in the heart. What does this Word say to me today or what does the Lord want to say to me at this particular moment?

It can be useful to consult a Bible commentary. It is not necessary to spend much time studying the text, but it is important to take a moment in order to get an idea of what God really is saying and so avoid the risk of making the Word say what we want to hear.

Respond

The third traditional moment or ingredient of Lectio Divina is *oratio*, which means prayer. This is our response to the Word of God. You may wonder have the earlier moments not also been prayer? Of course. However, according to the ancient monks, from whom we have received Lectio Divina, prayer was understood as an opportunity for a heart to heart dialogue with God. The two previous moments: reading the Word and reflecting on it are really a preparation for this intimate conversation with God. This intimate dialogue can take place in the midst of our normal daily tasks and can easily interchange with moments of meditation. For example, while we are working, we could perhaps think about the passage of Scripture that we had chosen, or, like the monks of antiquity, we might choose to repeat some word or phrase so that the Word of God might take hold of our heart. We have to adapt ourselves to the circumstances of our lives. These words or our thoughts are aimed at touching our heart and starting a real dialogue with God. The conversation with the Lord can take many forms and is very personal. The psalms cover the whole spectrum of human emotion and they teach us that we can speak with God about anything. The goal of Lectio Divina is to open the human heart to God so that it might be transformed.

Spontaneous prayer sooner or later tends to diminish and silence becomes more and more normal. In the silence we leave a space for the Spirit of God to pray in us.

Rest

The traditional name for the fourth moment or ingredient of Lectio Divina is *contemplatio* or contemplation. This is a concept with a lot of history behind it and not a few difficulties connected to it. I prefer to use a more common term that is easily understandable: rest. At this point we are invited to enter into the mystery of God. It is no longer necessary to think holy thoughts, or to speak but simply to rest in God.

> *Come to me, all you who labour and are overburdened, and I will give you rest. Shoulder my yoke and learn from me, for I am gentle and humble in heart, and you will find rest for your souls. Yes, my yoke is easy and my burden light. (Mt. 11, 28-30)*

When our prayer becomes silence, perhaps it may seem that we are wasting time. There will be a temptation to return to a form of prayer where we were in control, or at least where we had the sensation of doing something. However silence is a normal development of prayer. There comes a time when we must leave behind our beautiful words because they cannot express what is in our heart. In silence, God can listen to what is in our heart and we can listen to the still small voice of God.

According to the Catechism of the Catholic Church,

> 2713. *Contemplative prayer is the simplest expression of the mystery of prayer. It is a gift, a grace; it can be accepted only in humility and poverty. Contemplative prayer is a covenant relationship established by God within our hearts.*
>
> 2716. *It participates in the "Yes" of the Son become servant and the Fiat of God's lowly handmaid.*

When we read the Word of God, or meditate on it or pray about it, we are using our own words and thoughts, but the Word belongs to God and possibly God wants to comment on it. God often does this by inspiring a thought or a feeling. Sometimes God communicates by silence. The ancient monks believed that it was important to leave some time for God, and they called this time: *contemplatio*, contemplation.

The fruit of prayer is not the brilliant ideas that we may have about Scripture or the feelings of love that rise up in our heart. At times it is impossible to have a single holy thought. The fruit of prayer can only be seen outside the time of prayer in the way we relate with others on a regular basis. If our prayer is authentic, our life will begin to change, probably not in extraordinary ways, but in the small details of daily life. It is quite possible that we ourselves may not be at all aware of any of these changes, but they will begin to become clear to those with whom we live and work.

We need some quiet time when we leave behind our own words, thoughts, and ideas and simply rest in God, who loves us with a love that goes beyond anything we could imagine.

The dark night

The moments of Lectio Divina as a structure for the whole of life that models the movement into intimacy are prayer as a response from the heart and resting in God. In a human relationship this phase is a vast one from the exhilaration of falling in love to the stability of a mature love. One of the most striking elements of Carmelite prayer is the dark night that has been explained in great detail in terms of the progress in prayer by St. John of the Cross, and modelled in the concrete reality of daily life by St. Thérèse of Lisieux. According to St. John of the Cross, contemplation begins when God brings a beginner into the dark night of sense. [x] Contemplation is an inflow of God into the soul or when the person is brought further into the mystery of God. The night is dark because it is an encounter with God who is so dazzling that all we are aware of is darkness. John normally writes in terms of the life of prayer but contemplation and the dark night develop also within daily life. We can see this in the example of St. Thérèse, whose desire to stand in the truth was granted by the Lord. Before she entered Carmel, heaven was more real than earth and God was simply there. She could not understand atheists until her simple faith was taken away from her and she was exposed to excruciating doubt. She was content to share the table with sinners if that was where the Lord wanted her.[11] By means of this experience she matured in faith and so stood in the truth in relationship to God. She accepted God as God is and allowed the image of God that she had shaped to disappear.

Peter's experience that we have referred to previously, especially the scene where he confesses his faith in Jesus as the Son of God and then is told that he is a stumbling block to God's will, was an experience of dark night. By means of this harsh experience he was led to a new level of faith but first he had to learn the painful lesson that his all too human ideas could not define God; instead he had to let go of these ideas and allow God to teach him directly.

Elijah's experience sitting under the furze bush (1 Kings 19, 1-4) was also a kind of dark night. His faith had been completely vindicated. He was right and "his" God was the real God. Elijah had to learn that God was in fact beyond his limited ideas and that even such a great prophet did not have the full picture. Elijah is invited to go on the long journey, strengthened by food from heaven, to encounter God in a new way. God acts outside and beyond Elijah's understanding of who God is. God is not in the earthquake, or the mighty wind or the great fire but instead comes to the prophet in the sound of a gentle breeze or in the sound of sheer silence (1 Kings 19, 9-13). Elijah has got to adjust his own image of God and this experience must pass through the valley of darkness and doubt.[12]

The process of contemplation purifies our way of loving until we are transformed, able to see as God sees and love as God loves. We may think that we are very holy when we start off on the spiritual journey because we say some prayers and so on but in fact we are still very much focused on self. St. Teresa said that God walks amongst the pots and pans,[13] which means that God is at work very much in daily life. Therefore the process of transformation takes place also in the midst of daily life. For example when the honeymoon shine wears off in a relationship or when illness occurs, then we are challenged to refocus ourselves. The false self, which is focused on self-gratification, and can use even "holy" pursuits, like prayer for itself, is challenged by God in and through the events of life, so that we will move our basic orientation away from self to God, in whom alone we can find our true self. A good sign that we are acting out of the false self is if we are absolutely sure that we are not!

Silent Prayer

Prayer is essentially a personal relationship, a dialogue between God and the human person. We are invited to cultivate it and to find time and space to be with the Lord. Friendship can only grow through *"frequent one-to-one encounters with the One whom we know loves us"*, according to St. Teresa of Avila[14]. The Ratio goes on to say that beyond all matters of the form of prayer, what is important is to cultivate a deep friendship with Christ. It quotes St. Teresa once again in saying that perfect prayer *"does not consist in thinking much but in loving much"*.[15] The Constitutions remind us that: *"Silent prayer is of the greatest assistance in developing a spirit of contemplation; we should therefore practice it daily for an appropriate length of time."* (Art. 80).

So what is silent prayer and what is an appropriate length of time? We all lead very busy lives but we need to set priorities. Prayer is absolutely essential. The length of time depends on the individual's relationship with God and to a certain extent on one's creativity in finding the space and the time.

Every relationship has its own rhythm but usually over a period of time a relationship tends to become less complicated as the two people become more used to each other's ways. When you do not know a person very well, it is difficult to sit in silence with him or her. You tend to chat and to search for topics of conversation. As you grow to know the person better, the relationship becomes easier and sitting in companionable silence becomes normal and pleasant. When we become really attuned to another person we can begin to read his or her silences. In an intimate relationship, silence can be more eloquent than many words.

It is very normal over the course of time for our prayer to become more and more simple. It may be that we already have a little word or phrase that encapsulates all that we want to say to God. Saying this word means a thousand things. Jesus opened his heart to his disciples and shared with us the special name he had for God. This name is of course "Abba". This word contains the whole relationship of Jesus and the Father. It is very helpful to work out our own shorthand with God so that throughout the day we can remember the constant presence of God with us by repeating a simple word or phrase.

Each relationship with the Lord is different. If you get a lot out of sitting and chatting with the Lord, or meditating on a theme or reading and thinking about a passage of Scripture or reflecting on a spiritual book, that is fine. Please continue to do so. However there can be moments in a journey of prayer when a person becomes a bit stuck and is looking where to go next. It is also quite common to be led into silence during prayer and at first this can be quite strange and even frightening. We do not know what to do and we can feel that we are wasting our time. The great temptation is to give up prayer because we no longer find the consolation we once did and to give in to the feeling that it is a waste of time. St. Teresa of Avila strongly urges us not to give in to this temptation and to have a "great and very determined determination"[16] to stick with prayer especially when it is not going according to our plans.

It is a very common experience to undergo prolonged periods of dryness in prayer. Once again we often feel like giving up or we are upset and feel that God has gone away and not left a forwarding address. If we are somehow convinced of the value of prayer even in the midst of confusion and aridity, we might just sit in the dust waiting for God. On the very odd occasions that a holy thought comes floating down the river of our consciousness, we tend to pounce on it and throttle the life out of it, sucking it dry because we are parched. However there is another way of dealing with these very occasional holy thoughts. No matter how holy they may seem to be, they are *our* thoughts so it has been suggested that we let them come and let them go. If they are truly from God, then they will return at another time.

There are various methods for waiting in silence for God. I want to propose a method of prayer, which can make silence very fruitful and can help us wait for God in silence. It is a method of Christian prayer that is based on the very rich contemplative tradition and especially on a classic book of this tradition, *"The Cloud of Unknowing"*, written anonymously in the 14th century. I am not suggesting that one should leave other personal ways of prayer, but this method could deepen these other methods and make them even more fruitful. The most important thing for this way of prayer is to be convinced that God is not far away but is very close. God is at home within is. (cf. Jn. 14,23)

This method of prayer is can be called the prayer of silence or the prayer of desire because in the silence, we stretch out towards God with our desire. It has also been called centering prayer or prayer in secret, following Jesus' counsel to go into one's private room and to pray to the Father in secret. (Mt. 6,6).[17] The first phase of this prayer is to find a suitable place where the interruptions will be reduced to a minimum. Then get into a comfortable position that you can hold without fidgeting for the whole time of the prayer. Usually a minimum of 20 minutes is recommended. Now is not the time to think about the meaning of a passage of Scripture or a truth of the faith. That kind of meditation is for another time. Now is the time simply to be in the presence of God and consent to the divine action with our intention. Then, with eyes closed, introduce very gently a sacred word into the heart. A sacred word is a word that is very significant for you in your ongoing relationship with God. The sacred word should be sacred for you. According to the teaching of the "*Cloud of Unknowing* ", it is better if this word be very brief, one syllable if possible. I can suggest some possible words_ "God, Lord, Love, Jesus, Spirit, Father, Mary, Yes". Choose a word that is most significant for you. Perhaps one will come to you if you ask God's help.

Introducing the sacred word into one's heart does not mean to pronounce it with your lips, or even mentally, but welcome it within you without thinking of its meaning. It is not necessary to force the sacred word. It should be very gentle. The sacred word is not a mantra to be constantly repeated. The word focuses our desire and we use it always in the same way simply to return our heart to the Lord as soon as we become aware that we are distracted. By distracted I mean when we discover that we are engaged with any particular thought instead of simply being in the presence of God. This is a prayer of intention and not attention. Our intention is to be in the presence of God and to consent to the divine action in our lives. The sacred word expresses this intention and so when we become aware that we are thinking of something else, we can decide either to continue with this thought because we find it more interesting or return to our intention to be in the presence of God and consent to what God wants to accomplish in us. We return our heart to God by the very gentle use of the sacred word. It is a symbol of our intention. It is not necessary to repeat it frequently but only when we wish to return our heart to God. During the time of prayer thoughts will come but they need not be distractions if we let them come and let them go. As soon as we focus on some other thought, whether to fight it or get annoyed with ourselves because we are not doing what we think we should, then it becomes a distraction. The antidote is always the same – return ever so gently to the sacred word as the symbol of our intention to consent to God's presence and action.

During this prayer, it is not the time to talk to God with beautiful words or even to have holy thoughts, even if we think that these are inspirations from God. These things are best left for another moment. Our silence and our desire are worth far more than many words.

By means of the sacred word that we have chosen, we express our desire and our intention to remain in the presence of God and to consent to the purifying and transforming divine action. We return to the sacred word, which is the symbol of our intention and our desire, only when we become aware that we are involved in something else. The prayer consists simply in being in the presence of God without thinking of anything in particular. If you understand how to be in silence with another person without thinking or doing anything in particular, then you will be able to understand what this prayer is all about. This method of prayer is not for everyone. If you feel an interior call to greater silence, it may be of help to you.

At the end of the period that you have decided to dedicate to prayer, perhaps you can say an Our Father or other prayer very slowly. It is good to remain in silence for a few moments in order to prepare yourself to bring the fruit of your prayer into your daily life.

Practical guidelines for the Prayer in Secret

1. Choose a sacred word as the symbol of your intention to consent to the presence and action of God within.
2. Sitting comfortably and with eyes closed, settle briefly and silently introduce the sacred word as the symbol of your consent to God's presence and action within.
3. When engaged with your thoughts, return ever so gently to the sacred word
4. At the end of the prayer period, remain in silence with eyes closed for a couple of minutes.

Questions for Reflection

Personal: Are you faithful to a rhythm of public and personal prayer
Group: How can the prayer life of the community / Province / Congregation be improved?

Endnotes

1 Cf. KEITH J. EGAN, ed., *Carmelite Prayer. A Tradition for the 21st Century* (Paulist Press, New York, 2003).
2 ST. TERESA OF AVILA, *Interior Castle*, 1,7.
3 *Life*, 13, 13.
4 *Interior Castle*, 4,1, 7.
5 *The Practice of the Presence of God: The Best Rule of Holy Life*, compiled by Joseph de Beaufort after Lawrence's death.
6 *Gaudium et Spes. The Church in the Modern World*, 43.
7 The full text of this letter can be found in Appendix One of my book, *Mary the Contemplative* (Edizioni Carmelitane, Rome, 2001).
8 Cf. JOSEPH CHALMERS, *Let it Be*, (St. Albert's Press, expected 2010). This is an examination of all the texts in the New Testament relating to Mary in order to use them for prayer.
9 Cf. KLEMENS STOCK, *Mary the Mother of the Lord in the New Testament*, (Carmel in the World Paperbacks, 12, Edizioni Carmelitane, Rome, 2006), p. 117-120.
10 *Ascent of Mount Carmel*, II, 6,8.
11 *Story of a Soul*, Manuscript C, 6r.
12 Cf. JOSEPH CHALMERS, *The Sound of Silence. Listening to the Word of God with Elijah the Prophet*, (St. Albert's Press & Edizioni Carmelitane, 2007).
13 *Foundations*, 5, 8.

14 Life 8,5.
15 Foundations, 5,2; Interior Castle 4,1,7; RIVC, 31.
16 *Way of Perfection* 21, 2.
17 The fundamental handbook for this way of prayer is: Thomas Keating, *Open Mind, Open Heart, The Contemplative Dimension of the Gospel* (Element, Shaftesbury, Dorset, 1991, first published in 1986). For a simple introduction to this method of prayer, see ELIZABETH SMITH and JOSEPH CHALMERS, *A Deeper Love. An Introduction to Centering Prayer* (Continuum, New York & London, 1999).

CARMEL: A LIGHT IN THE DARKNESS

The hermits, who went to Mount Carmel, left their homes in Europe for many reasons. Perhaps they wanted to experience the excitement of the Crusades, or maybe they were doing penance for some sin. Whatever the reason, individually they decided to make their home on Mount Carmel in order to live in allegiance to Jesus Christ as hermits in holy penitence.

Europe was in turmoil in the late 12th and early 13th centuries and there were many religious movements. We no longer use the term "fuga mundi" that the hermits might have used. We do not like the idea that we might be running away from the world. However at the time of the hermits, "fuga mundi" did not have the negative connotation that we tend to put upon it. The early monks and hermits left the world in order to go into the desert, which was understood to be the stronghold of the demons. They went into the desert not to have a quiet, peaceful life, away from the problems of the world, but to fight against the Evil One who *"is on the prowl like a roaring lion looking for prey to devour"* (I Pet. 5,8; Rule 18). In order to take part in this battle, they needed to have strong armour. This is why our Rule tells us to put on the armour of God in order to be ready to withstand the enemy's ambush (Rule 18).

The hermits followed this particular way of living in allegiance to Jesus Christ, because they wanted to bring light into the darkness and so overcome the Evil One. They were responding to a call from God. Their decisions have shaped our lives profoundly and gave birth to what has become the great Carmelite Family present in every continent. We have very different ways of imaging the spiritual life and we face very different problems, according to where we live and minister, but our vocation is fundamentally the same, as outlined by our Rule. We have to take on the fundamental Carmelite values as contained in our Rule and filled out by the history of the Order and the lives of concrete Carmelites, especially our saints and great theologians. With these fundamental Carmelite values, we have to face our sometimes very different world. Our Constitutions express for our times what the Order considers to be the fundamental Carmelite values.

In the Constitutions the Order says: *"Carmelites live their life of allegiance to Christ through a commitment to seek the face of the living God (the contemplative dimension of life), through fraternity, and through service in the midst of the people."* (Const. 14). The Constitutions go on to say that these values are united through the experience of the desert, which is one way of describing contemplation. Our mission in the Church is focused on promoting the search for God and the life of prayer (Const. 95). In our following of Christ today, we allow our lives to be shaped by the Word of God and we are inspired above all by the example of Our Lady and the Prophet Elijah.

We are to co-operate with Jesus Christ in his work of bringing humanity into the Reign of God. We do this through all the different ministries in which we are involved. The great work of Christ is proclaiming the Good News from God through his preaching but above all by means of his death and resurrection. He brings salvation, which is the transformation of humanity into the image and likeness of God and the transformation of our world, according to God's will. Jesus told the people in the synagogue of Nazareth that he had come to proclaim Good News to the poor. (Lk. 4, 16-21). The prophets had various ways of visualising the messianic era of peace and justice when the Good News would be fulfilled. Isaiah foretold,

A shoot shall sprout from the stump of Jesse, and from his roots a bud shall blossom.

2 The spirit of the LORD shall rest upon him: a spirit of wisdom and of understanding, A spirit of counsel and of strength, a spirit of knowledge and of fear of the LORD,

3 and his delight shall be the fear of the LORD. Not by appearance shall he judge, nor by hearsay shall he decide,

4 But he shall judge the poor with justice, and decide aright for the land's afflicted. He shall strike the ruthless with the rod of his mouth, and with the breath of his lips he shall slay the wicked.

5 Justice shall be the band around his waist, and faithfulness a belt upon his hips.

6 Then the wolf shall be a guest of the lamb, and the leopard shall lie down with the kid; The calf and the young lion shall browse together, with a little child to guide them.

> *7 The cow and the bear shall be neighbors, together their young shall rest; the lion shall eat hay like the ox.*
> *8 The baby shall play by the cobra's den, and the child lay his hand on the adder's lair.*
> *9 There shall be no harm or ruin on all my holy mountain; for the earth shall be filled with knowledge of the LORD, as water covers the sea. (Is. 11, 1-9).*

We are called to take part in this great work of bringing about the fulfillment of the plan of God for our world. In order to be effective co-workers with Christ, we must allow the grace of God to transform our own hearts. Transformation is not just an external change of one or two details but is a profound change of how we relate to others, to the world and to God. We cannot do so without undergoing a process of transformation ourselves.

Transformation in Christ

The RIVC, or Ratio, the formation document of the Carmelite Order, speaks very powerfully about this process of transformation, which is both individual and collective:

> *Through this gradual and continuous transformation in Christ, which is accomplished within us by the Spirit, God draws us to himself on an inner journey which takes us from the dispersive fringes of life to the inner core of our being, where he dwells and where he unites us with himself.*
> *This requires a constant, radical and lifelong effort, through which, inspired by God's grace, we begin to think, judge, and*

> *re-order our lives, in accordance with God's holiness and goodness as revealed and poured out in abundance in the Son. This process is neither linear nor uniform. It involves critical moments, crises in growth and in maturation, stages where we must make new choices - especially when we have to renew our option for Christ. All this is part of the purification of our spirits at the deepest level, by which we may be conformed to God.*
>
> *The inner process which leads to the development of the contemplative dimension helps us to acquire an attitude of openness to God's presence in life, teaches us to see the world with God's eyes, and inspires us to seek, recognise, love and serve God in those around us. (RIVC, 24)*

All of this work of personal and communitarian transformation is taking place in a world that is so obviously full of problems and injustice. The spiritual journey is not a flight from the world in the negative sense but is a withdrawal from certain aspects of life – marriage, family, career, etc. depending on our particular state in life, in order to concentrate our limited forces on the same war in which the first Carmelites were involved. We must be fully involved in the world in order to co-operate with Christ for its transformation.

Human beings and human structures cause many of the problems of our world. History tells us that if a war is concluded with a peace that oppresses one party, it simply lays the foundations for the next war. We have also seen many wars in our own day having their roots in some injustice hundreds of years before. We cannot resolve the problems of our world. However, it is possible to throw ourselves into our work in such a way that we simply add to the din, being part of the problem and not part of the solution. We must allow the Gospel to question our values and our motives. Are our values really Gospel values? Are our values the same as the fundamental Carmelite values? Are our motives pure? This can be a very painful process as we begin to see ourselves as we really are.

In order to really be part of the solution, we must actively enter into the process of transformation by means of which God transforms our world but this involves our personal transformation too. We cannot have one without the other. Therefore, like the first Carmelite hermits, we too must go into the desert to face the demons that dwell there. The demons I am thinking about are those within the human heart. The desert is not necessarily a particular place but a situation by means of which God speaks to our heart and in which we do not have our normal means of escape. These desert situations bring us face to face with who we are. We are of course good because the good God has created us but we are marked by the Fall – the human condition and our personal sin. It is not sufficient to repent of our sins; the roots must be pulled up, i.e. what has caused us to act in such a way. Our times are marked by a loss of a sense of sin, so perhaps instead of looking for the causes of our sins, whatever they may be, we could look at what motivates us throughout the whole of our life. Caritas Christi urget nos? Are we really motivated by the love of Christ? Are we perhaps motivated by other, less elevated motives? Look at

Carmel: A Light in the Darkness

your likes and dislikes; look at your powerful emotions – your anger, your feelings of rejection and so on. Try to name some of these and bring them out into the light. Where do these come from? What are the causes of these emotions and the behaviour that sometimes is based on them?

We have a common vocation as Carmelites. We are in this together. We need the support of each other. If we are going to help one another, each of us has to go into the desert and face our own demons whatever they may be and they will be different for each of us. If we do not walk into the desert willingly, we will be taken there at some point in our lives and that can be much more difficult. Protected by the armour provided by God, we need to fight against all that is false within us and all that adds to the problems of the world. The falsity within us can be very subtle and often hides under a veneer of religiosity so that it is not brought out into the light and seen for what it is.

Just as the hermits left their homes for many reasons, so the same could be said for us. We wanted to become Carmelites but we did not fully understand all that this choice implied. This became clear as we were able to face up to each stage of our human and religious development. The Carmelite journey is a journey towards transformation. Walking this path, we consciously enter into a process of purification of our motives that lie behind what we do and what we say in daily life.

Prayer is essential for this journey. As the RIVC says:

> *In prayer we open ourselves to God, who, by his action, gradually transforms us through all the great and small events of our lives. This process of transformation enables us to enter into and sustain authentic fraternal relationships; it makes us willing to serve, capable of compassion and of solidarity, and gives us the ability to bring before the Father the aspirations, the anguish, the hopes and the cries of the people.*
>
> *Fraternity is the testing ground of the authenticity of the transformation which is taking place within us. We discover that we are brothers journeying towards the one Father, sharing the gifts of the Spirit and supporting one another through the hardships of the journey. (RIVC, 23).*

Dealing with darkness

As we walk the path of transformation, we will at some point have to deal with darkness. The dark night, both in its active and passive dimensions, according to John of the Cross, refers to the growth in one's relationship with God. It is caused by the impact of God on the human person. God is like a blinding light. It takes our eyes a long time to become adjusted and until they do, we are in darkness. The bright light of God shows up all the dust that was not visible under a normal light. In the light of God we see ourselves as we really are, which is not always a very pleasant experience, because we see all our pettiness, the illusions, the mixed motives and so on. The dark night is a good sign that one is moving forward on the spiritual journey. John calls it "a blessed night" because it is the sign of God's powerful presence and action in our lives.

Depression is something different from the dark night, though it may be part of the total experience.[1] Even though depression may be part of the experience of the dark night, it has to be treated differently. A spiritual director is usually not the person to treat clinical depression. The "blues" are part of every life and feeling down from time to time is not necessarily a sign of clinical depression or of the dark night. God is in every experience, whether it is pleasant or unpleasant, and every experience can teach us something about God and about the spiritual journey.

The Prophet Elijah

I want to approach this topic of dealing with darkness from the perspective of two important biblical figures. Firstly I want to look at what we might learn from the experience of the Prophet Elijah. What is now known as the Carmelite Rule was initially written as a letter from St. Albert, the Patriarch of Jerusalem, between 1206 and 1214, to the hermits who live by the spring on Mount Carmel. The Prophet Elijah was known as the model for all monks and hermits and the first Carmelite hermits could not have been unaware of his connection with the place they had chosen to establish their monastery. This spring on Mount Carmel was known as Elijah's spring and is still there today. Jews, Christians and Muslims still go there on pilgrimage to honour the prophet. He has exercised a strong influence on Carmelite spirituality throughout the centuries.

This austere prophet, remained alive in the people's memory to the point that there arose dramatic and miraculous stories about him. From the end of the 9th century B.C.E, can be found a series of stories concerning Elijah. These stories were conserved and spread above all during the great Exile, when the people found themselves in a situation without hope, seemingly abandoned. They lived daily with frustration, destruction and in a state of utter confusion. Several times the people of Israel had suffered deportation after defeat in war. However, the deportation to Babylonia left a lasting and profound impact on the soul of the people. It seemed that God had renounced the plan of salvation whereby God had brought the people out of the slavery of Egypt into the Promised Land. After the deportations, many believed that the situation would only last a short while, but that was an illusion. The stories about Elijah helped the exiles to understand something of their situation, notwithstanding the official attempts to interpret events in a totally different way. On returning from exile, the people began to speak of the ancient prophets as the ones who had given them hope, and in a particular way, this hope centred on the Prophet Elijah.

The context of the stories about Elijah in the books of the Kings (I Kings 17-21 and 2 Kings 1-2) is the account of the struggle in Israel against religious syncretism, that is many Israelites had confused the worship of the true God, Yahweh, with that of the idol Baal. The neighbours of Israel all had many gods but Israel had only one God. He had given His people this command: - *"You shall have no god except me"* (Dt.5,7).

However as time passed, the Israelites settled down as farmers in their new land and they began to accept many of the customs from their highly civilised pagan neighbours. Idol worshipping became prevalent in Israel. The worship of idols flourishes today. The names of the idols have changed but the reality is the same. There is the gross idolatry of the modern world for materialism but there is also the insidious idolatry to which Christians can be prone. The Pharisees in Jesus' day seemed to have sincerely believed that they were serving God but Jesus castigated them for paying lip service only while their hearts were in fact far from God. How many Christians profess to believe while their lives go against their words? When we have some sort of negative experience in our lives, it is worthwhile asking ourselves, why is it that we feel bad. Is it because some idol, perhaps dressed in a holy way, is being challenged?

The prophet Elijah appeared on the scene at a very critical moment in Israel's history. Ahab, the king of Israel, married Jezebel, the princess of Tyre. She was a worshipper of the idol Baal among others. When she married, she brought with her over 800 prophets and priests of her religion. She seemed to be determined to convert the whole of Israel to her more "civilised" religion. She was determined to impose her "advanced" culture on the barbarous people her husband ruled over. At some stage Queen Jezebel began persecuting the followers of Yahweh and she succeeded in driving resistance underground. It was the prophet Elijah who brought together the opposition to Jezebel.

Elijah appears on the scene with only the minimum of introduction to announce the beginning of a great drought (I Kings 17,1). This drought is the judgement of Yahweh, the God of Israel, because of the unfaithfulness of the people. According to his worshippers, one of Baal's great gifts was the rain, which is so necessary for the crops. So this is a direct challenge to the authority of the idol. We are naturally unhappy when we do not get what we want. Have we been looking for it in the wrong place?

The king accused Elijah of being a source of trouble for Israel but the prophet denied this and said that it was the king himself who was causing all the trouble. A prophet does cause trouble but only because he upsets those who reject God in their hearts no matter what the external appearances may be. A good example of this is Archbishop Romero of El Salvador, whose whole approach changed when he saw the suffering of the ordinary people. His own priests and catechists were being killed for trying to help the people in their sufferings. He then began to preach the Gospel without compromise and naturally he aroused the fury of those who were in power. The powerful ones sought the blessing of the Church for what they were doing but Romero refused to go along with oppression and he suffered for this.

Elijah challenged the people and so the famous

contest on Mount Carmel took place (1 Kings 18, 20-39). This was to decide who was God in Israel - Yahweh or Baal. It was an either - or contest. As Elijah said to the people gathered on Mount Carmel, *"Stop hobbling about first on one foot and then on the other. If Yahweh is God, then follow Him. If Baal is God, then follow him"* (1 Kings 18, 21). With God there can be no compromise. We cannot serve two masters. What faith Elijah must have had to propose this contest! We are told that if we had faith even as small as a grain of mustard seed, we could move mountains. Faith is a commitment of our whole being into the darkness of God who has revealed Himself to us in Jesus, His Son. Often we must continue to trust in the darkness despite all appearances to the contrary.

The story describes the contest. There are to be two sacrifices but whoever responds with fire to the prayers is God in Israel. Elijah was obviously very polite and he gave the first attempt to the priests of Baal. No matter how many prayers they said or how often they cut themselves in a frenzy, there was no response from Baal. Elijah enjoyed the discomfiture of his opponents and made helpful suggestions that perhaps the reason for Baal's lack of response was that he was busy or perhaps he had gone on a journey or perhaps he had fallen asleep or even gone to the toilet! (I Kings 18, 27). Then finally Elijah took over and he prepared his sacrifice making it very clear that there were no tricks involved (1 Kings 18, 30-36). He repaired an altar to God and laid his sacrifice upon it. We are told that in response to Elijah's prayer fire came down from heaven and consumed the sacrifice. The people were most impressed by this and declared as one, *"the Lord is God! The Lord is God!"* (1 Kings 18, 39). It is impossible from this distance to know what exactly happened on Mount Carmel but that something did seems fairly certain because Elijah won a great victory against his enemies and the enemies of God. As was the custom in those days, he had the priests and prophets of the idol slaughtered and he announced to the king an end to the drought that God had imposed on the country for its infidelity. However Elijah does not have much time to enjoy the fruits of victory because Jezebel, the Queen, is most unhappy and sends a message in which she threatens to kill him and the great faith and confidence he displayed in the contest of Mount Carmel vanishes very quickly. He runs away and finally, in the desert, he sits down under the bush and wishes he were dead I Kings 19, 1-4).

The Crisis

God approaches us in many ways and helps us to grow. The growth can be very gradual but we can take a big step by really trying to hear His voice and responding to Him in the midst of a crisis in our lives. Is God asking me to let go of some cherished notion or do I need to move on and leave behind something that was good at a certain period of my life but no longer can help me on my journey towards God? What is the reason for the crisis and why do I feel it to be a crisis? What is going on inside of me? Sometimes we blame other people for our difficulties and we miss what God wants to say to us.

Elijah felt completely alone in the desert and had no more strength to carry on the battle against the idolatry of Baalism. Yet God does not let Elijah sink into self-pity. He has further work for the prophet to do and He sends His angel twice to encourage Elijah by making him eat and drink to strengthen him for the journey to Horeb, the mountain of God.

Perhaps at times in our lives we have felt something like Elijah felt in the desert. What is the point of carrying on? I seem to take one step forward and two steps back. Where is God? Why do I never experience His presence like others seem to do? What is wrong with me? Crisis is part of our lives; it is part of being human. It is not bad to go through times of doubt and questioning, it is normal. However the important thing is how we cope with crises. Elijah just wanted to lie down and die. He used sleep as an escape from the pressures of reality. We too can often seek to escape the problems of life and the methods of escape are numerous. I think that a crisis in our life is intended to lead us to a deeper level of reality. A crisis means a turning point or a decisive moment in our lives. It is a call from God to enter more deeply into Him by discovering Him in the depths of our own being. Why then do we try to run away? I think that we try to run away from God at times because we receive a little taste of the complete Otherness of God and His absolute demands. Can I really throw myself into the unfathomable Abyss of God? Will I not lose everything?

We do not like to think this way and so we can have very subtle ways of attempting to escape God. We try to manipulate God and the divine will to suit our own purposes. We are prepared to love God and do God's will so long as we remain in control of what goes on. We say all sorts of things to God but when we have to make a major decision, we are not prepared to give away everything and stand naked before the presence of the Ultimate Mystery we call God because we would then be totally out of control.

God is a demanding God, a jealous God. He will have no other gods before Him. God's love and God's presence burn. Nothing can live in this presence, which is not God. If we do throw ourselves into the furnace of God's love and accept that we are no longer in control, there will take place a great purification process in which all impurities will be burned away. The purpose of this purification is to transform us from within so that we become quite literally God-like. This process is of course painful but the witness of the great saints testifies that it is worth it.

God had to send His angel twice to Elijah before he would move. An angel is a messenger from God. These messengers come in all shapes and sizes. Can we recognise God's angels when they come to us? Sometimes the visit of God's messengers is not at all comforting. Remember the struggle that Jacob had with the angel (Gen. 32, 26-30). They wrestled all night and Jacob came away from the struggle with a wound, which was a constant reminder to him of the occasion. The wound that we receive in our struggle with God can be a great blessing. St. John of the Cross wrote:

> *Where can your hiding be,*
> *Beloved, that you left me thus to moan*
> *While like the stag you flee*
> *Leaving the wound with me?*
> *I followed calling loud but you had flown.*[2]

Elijah carried on his journey to Horeb. When he arrives there, he has to answer a question. God asks him, *"Elijah, what are you doing here?"* (I Kings 18,9, 9). Elijah tells God that he is filled with jealous zeal for the Lord God of hosts. Elijah thinks that he is the only one left who is faithful to the true God and his enemies are out to kill him. He learns later than in fact there are over 7,000 people who have not bent the knee to Baal. Elijah has to learn that God is not totally dependent on Elijah; instead the success of Elijah's mission depends totally on the power of God.

Does God depend on us to get things done? What would God do without us? The story of Gideon is very instructive. (Jgs.7) He is about to go into battle against Midian with an army of 32,000. According to God that is far too many lest they think that they had won the battle with their own strength. The army is whittled down to 300 and they win a great victory due to God's power. The success of our ministry does not depend on our power but on God. The success of anything we do cannot be judged by external factors but only by God.

Elijah is told to go and stand outside on the mountain and there God makes his appearance. God does not come in the mighty wind or the earthquake or the fire but *"in the sound of a gentle breeze"* or *"in the sound of silence"* (1 Kgs. 19,12). The Hebrew text seems to be a bit different from the Greek translation. In the Hebrew the noise is more insistent even stunning. God did not come to Elijah in the way the prophet expected. God comes to us in unexpected ways too. Can we hear the sound of a gentle breeze or the sound of silence? Are we prepared to be stunned into silence? There have been various interpretations of the sound. Some say that the point is God works through the ordinary events of life and that Elijah should not expect another miracle like that on Mt. Carmel. Can we hear the voice of God? Can we discern the presence of God in the midst of the events, which happen to us every day? At times do we look in the wrong places for God? God responded to Elijah's prayer on Mount Carmel but Elijah has to learn that God cannot be controlled. We must be prepared to accept God as He chooses to reveal Himself to us. Often God chooses humble ways to approach us, so humble that we can let Him slip by without noticing His presence. If God came to us like an earthquake, we couldn't help but notice. But no, God comes to us like the sound of a gentle breeze or in the sound of silence. God is just as much present in the insignificant details of our lives as in the major events. Let us ask God to open our eyes and our hearts so that we might be awake to see Him when He comes.

Faithful and Creative

After this appearance of God on Mount Horeb, Elijah returns to the more mundane facts of daily life. Even if we do have a deep experience of God's presence, we must return to our ordinary lives. Faithfulness to God is not proved in the religious high points but in the very ordinary things we do every day. The ordinary is filled with the divine presence if only we have the eyes to see.

Next Elijah discovers that Ahab and Jezebel have killed Naboth (1 Kings 21) in order to obtain his vineyard. Elijah pronounces the judgement of the Lord, which leads to Ahab's repentance. Elijah is ready to speak God's word in season and out of season. There are times when we would rather not hear God's word, which comes to us not only through the Scriptures but also through one another. Also the word of God that Elijah speaks is not just pious doctrine but always has an effect. We are a word from God. We must seek to incarnate in our lives the values of God's Word so that our lives too may be effective witnesses to the presence of God in the world.

Two attitudes of Elijah stand out from all the stories about him. He was intensely faithful to the true God of Israel and he was also creative. The real danger in Israel at the time of Elijah was not that people would switch allegiance en masse from Yahweh to the idol Baal but that they would make an idol out Yahweh, the true God. We are made in the image of God. An idol is made in our image and is a god whom we can control. We, like Elijah, must be faithful to the true God, which involves a radical faith. We must accept the fact that we can never grasp God with our intellectual concepts. We must always seek to allow God to be God. We must be constantly aware of the danger of trying to manipulate God, of trying to turn Him into our servant. Like Elijah, we are servants of God (cf. 1 Kings 17, 1; 18,15).

Faithfulness to the true God goes hand in hand with creativity. Elijah actually changed the image of God, which the people had. God does not change but people do. The image of the Lord that was prevalent in the time of Elijah was outdated and so God seemed to have nothing to do with their lives. Elijah showed the people that the God of Israel was indeed relevant to their daily lives. He did not change God; he changed the idea of God which the people had.

As we grow up, our image of God changes. Some people who are very developed in many areas of their lives get stuck with an immature idea of God. We seek the face of the living God and we know that any image of God is not God. St. John of the Cross teaches us that we must be continually re-assessing our idea of God because He is beyond all our limited images and concepts. Therefore, like Elijah, we too must be faithful to the true God and have the courage to be creative in our relationship with Him.

We cannot cling on to outdated concepts, which have given us security in the past because our security can only be found in God. We are drawn ever forward into the future that God is creating out of our present. The future is unknown to us and therefore can appear to be frightening but we are asked to trust the One who has brought us so far.

Elijah was a prophet who lived in God's presence. The Word of God burned in Elijah and through him, God turned the hearts of the people back to Himself. The Word of God lives in us too. Does it burn in our hearts?[3]

The Call of the Disciple

Carmelite spirituality focuses on the relationship with God and our call to become transformed in God. Transformation is a process in which the human person becomes all he or she can be through the grace of God. We have been made in the image and likeness of God and so the vocation of each one of us is to become like God. This is a long road, a narrow road, that reaches its terminus only after the passage through death. It is important to remain on this road and not to become enticed onto other, perhaps superficially more attractive roads.

Carmelite spirituality speaks of the various stages that the human heart goes through on this long journey of faith.[4] First of all we have the stage of the longing heart, which is a recognition that there is something missing that would make our lives complete. We try to satisfy this longing in many ways, which can never satisfy us completely. Some people in our secularized societies seem not to be aware that there is anything in the spiritual sphere that is missing in their lives.

When one does wake up and recognise that there is something missing, this is the beginning of the spiritual journey. However we have to battle the continual temptation to stop on the road and settle for far less than we were created for. Our hearts have been created as deep caverns that can only be filled by the Infinite but we do not want to pay the price of receiving God in our lives. The heart can become enslaved to the worship of lesser gods.[5] These lesser gods or idols are any person, place or thing from which we seek the happiness that can come from God alone. We often try to satisfy the deep longings of our hearts with what is not God. These "lesser gods" can make us happy for a time but then we begin to look elsewhere. The danger is that we get sucked deeper and deeper into materialism and succeed in blocking off the still small voice of God.

Carmelite spirituality speaks especially about prayer because without this strong pillar we could not advance much on the spiritual journey. There is no single method of prayer that is laid down for Carmelites but great freedom is given to each person to find those ways that help one grow in relationship with God.[6] Carmel is of course synonymous with contemplation, which is not a method of prayer but a way of relating to God that is God's gift.[7] We can do whatever is possible for us to prepare for this gift especially by seeking to develop a listening heart. It is prayer that helps us on the journey of faith through the various ups and downs of life until our heart is purified of all that is not God.

All of us have to deal with darkness at different stages in our lives. There is darkness when we are letting go of "lesser gods" or "lesser loves" because we have found a deeper love. There is darkness when we are simply dealing with the sufferings that life throws up. These sufferings can embitter the soul or lead us further on our journey into God. St. Thérèse, at the same time that she was writing of her vocation to be "love in the heart of the Church", was also struggling with doubts about the existence of God. She felt nothing when she prayed and often fell asleep at her prayers and especially after communion. The rosary was excruciating for her. Her father, whom she loved greatly, descended into madness, and she had to cope with the suggestion that she was to blame. She also had incurable TB and faced death at the age of 24. What brought her through all this was her faith, that is her belief that God loved her despite being able to feel nothing.

Prayer throws light on previously unexamined corners of the soul. Prayer is not intended to make us feel holy but to lead us into a journey of discovery. St. Teresa of Avila says that the first fruit of authentic prayer is self-knowledge and indeed this must accompany our whole journey of faith.[8] Prayer will show us what is false within us; it will show us our inauthentic ways of living. Perhaps some people become frightened and think that they are better off not praying. Any relationship brings change to our lives. Those who are married or those of us who live in community know how much we have had to change in order to accommodate the other. So also in the relationship with Christ. Often it is delightful at the beginning, just like falling in love. Falling in love is easy; continuing to love is the hard part.

The life of the first Carmelites, who were hermits at the end of the 12th and the beginning of the 13th centuries, was based on Lectio Divina, the prayerful reading of the Word of God. The goal of Lectio Divina is to lead to contemplation, which is an intimate union of life with God. By getting to know the Word of God, we get to know Christ and gradually he leads us on the road towards our complete fulfillment: transformation in God. Lectio is a way of developing a close friendship with Christ. Friendship with Christ was the goal of the hermits on Mt. Carmel. It is the heart of the spirituality of St. Teresa of Avila and of the Little Way of St. Thérèse, even though neither had access to a complete copy of the Bible. Friendship with Christ is what gave Edith Stein and Titus Brandsma courage to lay down their lives in the face of Nazi persecution. Friendship with Christ is what brought all the Carmelite saints and an innumerable host of unknown people through times of difficulty and darkness.

The Rock

I want to apply these principles once again using a figure from the Scriptures to illustrate some more

Carmelite perspectives on the issue of dealing with darkness. One of my favourite characters from the New Testament is Peter. He had to deal with plenty of darkness in his growing friendship with Christ. How the Church grew and developed based on the apostles as they are shown in the Gospels is a great mystery and points to the fact that human beings can plant and water but it is God who grants the growth (cf. 1 Cor. 3, 6-9). Simon, who was later called Peter, was called by Jesus to follow him. Very generously he did so and began a great adventure. At some point each one of us was called to follow the Lord. Perhaps we can remember a specific moment and perhaps not. In St. Luke's Gospel there is an interesting slant on the call. Jesus steps into Simon's boat and directs him to a huge catch of fish. Peter is overwhelmed and says: "*Leave me Lord for I am a sinful man*" (Lk. 5,8). In the presence of the light we begin to become aware of our own darkness. When we allow God to shine a light within us, we become aware of our own sinfulness. One way of dealing with that experience is to run away and find something to divert you so that you do not have to think about things like that, or you can continue to allow the light to probe the dark corners of your life.

The Gospels tell us that it was Jesus who gave Simon another name - Peter. This has always intrigued me. Was this a joke? The new name meant Rock or perhaps Rocky! In the rest of the Gospel, Peter appears to be very rocky indeed. However Jesus saw something in him and called it out from him. This is an important element of the spiritual journey. When Jesus calls us, he looks at us and sees what is possible. We have not attained our destiny at the beginning of our journey and a lot of work needs to be done on us in order that we might become what we were created to be.

In Mark's Gospel we are given a snapshot of a day in the life of Jesus during the early period of his ministry when he had a great deal of success. (Mk. 1,21-39). We are told that the people were spellbound by his preaching. Jesus then went to Capharnaum where he began to heal people including Peter's mother-in-law. Peter was obviously a very close friend of this man and therefore would be expected to have some influence with him. The next morning Jesus is nowhere to be found. One of the translations tells us that Simon and his companions *"managed to track him down"*.[9] When they found Jesus, he was absorbed in prayer. It is impossible to know exactly what happened but it seems that the apostles were very excited and they broke in on Jesus' prayer to give him the momentous news that everyone was looking for him. They expected him to go back to produce another sell out show but instead Jesus invites them to walk away from the fame and glory and follow him: *"Let us move on to the neighbouring villages to proclaim the Good News there also. That is what I have come to do."* (Mk. 1,38).

What did Simon Peter feel at that point? Was he on a high and ready to become the agent or the manager for this wonder worker but instead he was reminded of his call to follow Jesus. The darkness that descended on Peter was for his healing and growth. Often we compartmentalise our lives: we have special times for God and then we have our ordinary lives where we just get on with living. However, every aspect of life is included in our relationship with God. I do not know if God causes everything that happens to us but certainly God is in the midst of everything, even the most seemingly insignificant events. God is calling us ever forward out of the prison of the false self towards the freedom of the children of God.[10] When things happen to stop us in our tracks and make us think about what we are doing, they may be objectively bad things but they are also graced moments. God speaks to us in and through the darkness and calls us to listen and follow the sound of the still small voice.

Gradually Jesus led the disciples on a journey of faith. He taught them; they witnessed many miracles, which were signs of the Kingdom of God already present. However they also experienced difficulties. They saw Jesus being rejected in his own hometown; John the Baptist was executed. However, gradually the disciples began to understand that Jesus was much more than John the Baptist. He did things that only God could do: he fed the multitude (Mt. 14, 15-21;Mk. 6,34-44; Lk. 9, 12-17), and he even walked on the water (Mt. 14, 22-33;Mk. 6, 45-52; Jn. 6, 6-21). Matthew's Gospel tells us specifically about Peter's reaction. Jesus sent the disciples ahead of him. Perhaps they wondered how he was going to get there as he had no boat. The disciples ran into a very heavy storm and were in great difficulties. They saw a ghostly figure walking towards them on the water and not unnaturally they were mightily afraid. Jesus quietened their fears by calling out, *"Take courage. Do not be afraid. It is I"* (Mt. 14, 27). Peter spoke up for the others. All of them were obviously very doubtful about this figure. Walking on the water was completely outside their experience, so Peter said to Jesus, *"Lord, if it is you, command me to come to you on the water"*. Perhaps Peter was a bit impetuous and did not really think about what he was saying. However Jesus told him to come across the water. We have to give credit to Peter; he got out of the boat and according to the story he actually started to walk to Jesus across the water. Please do not try this in deep water unless you are a very strong swimmer! Not surprisingly the intrepid Peter began to realize where he was and what he was doing. At that moment he became terrified and began to sink beneath the waves. He called out to Jesus, "Lord, save me!" Jesus caught hold of him and brought him safely back into the boat with the other disciples. *"Oh man of little faith,"* Jesus said to him, *"Why did you doubt?"* (Mt. 14, 32).

Peter had made a fool of himself in front of all the other apostles. The others were probably glad that it had happened to Peter and not to them. This must have been a dark moment in Peter's journey of faith. It was quite a public failure but it was also a moment of grace. When Jesus got in the boat, the disciples said, *"Truly, you are the Son of God"* (Mt. 14, 33).

On another occasion, Jesus asked the apostles what the people were saying about him. (Mt. 16,

13-20; Mk. 8, 27-33; Lk. 9, 18-21). There were all sorts of fantastic ideas going around and the disciples probably reported all this with many a laugh but then the laughter stopped when he asked them what was their opinion: "*And you, who do you say that I am?*" This question echoes down the centuries and each one of us is faced with it. Each of us must answer it individually. Who is Jesus for you? Is he the answer to the longings of your heart? Is he your closest and most intimate friend with whom you are willing to spend time in profound conversation? Peter answered for all the disciples: "*You are the Christ, the Son of the Living God.*" Matthew's Gospel is the one that brings out this scene most vividly. Jesus congratulates Peter: "*You are blessed Simon, Son of Jonah, for it was not flesh and blood that revealed this to you but my Father in heaven.*" Imagine how Peter felt being praised by Jesus, whom he believed to be the messiah, and in front of all the other apostles. Once Jesus has brought the disciples to take this step of faith, he now proceeds to reveal to them what it means to be the messiah. He is to be a suffering messiah.

Obviously the disciples do not like this. They are shocked by what Jesus has said. They all have a different view of what the messiah should be, and their view has some backing from their religious tradition. Peter, again the spokesman for the Twelve, takes Jesus aside and tells him in no uncertain terms that he might be the messiah but he is wrong. Peter rejects what Jesus has said very strongly. The word used in Mark's Gospel is a very strong term and indicates a fundamental opposition. However, equally strongly, Jesus rejects what Peter has said, and tells him that he is a satan, a stumbling block. Jesus is determined to do the will of the Father and he will not be diverted from it no matter how enticing the temptation may be. Imagine now what Peter must have felt. He must have been very sure of himself but he has been told very clearly that he is wrong. Peter must have been enveloped in darkness. He had to rethink his whole position with regard to Jesus. This darkness was once again for his healing. However, Peter could have walked away because what Jesus was proposing was too hard and did not follow his own opinion. It takes great courage to recognise that our god is made in our own image instead of us being made in God's image.

Finally the Gospels tell us about Peter's famous betrayal of the Master. Despite everything, Peter still suffers from over-confidence. *"Even though I should have to die with you, I will not deny you."* All the disciples said the same thing. (Mt. 26,35). All the Gospels record this scene (Mk. 14, 26-31; Lk. 22, 31-34; Jn. 13, Jn. 13, 36-38) and so it was obviously a very important memory for the Church. When the crunch came, they all deserted Jesus and Peter denied even ever having known him.

Peter was recognised to be the leader of the apostles but there was no attempt to cover up his human weakness. Jesus called him and gave him the name Peter, "the Rock", because he saw something in Simon that would, with some formation, make him ready to be a rock for the new community. Peter had to get in touch with his own darkness and allow Christ to bring light to those places. He did not know that he had darkness inside him; it was only through his growing relationship with Jesus that he came to recognise this darkness and how it could be healed.[11]

Through everything that happens to us, God is calling us out of the prison of the false self towards the freedom of the children of God where we can get in touch with our true selves. The false self is the part of ourselves that feels the need always to defend our own interests. It is not easy to let go of this self because it is the only self we believe there is. Therefore Jesus stressed that only those who let go of their lives, will receive them in abundance. If we were not challenged, we would never become aware of this false side and the many ways it has to defend its own interests. Even when we become interested in religious things, the false self is not destroyed, it simply shifts its focus to the religious world and seeks itself there.

Dealing with darkness is never easy but God is always in the midst of this darkness willing to lead us forward into the light.

Endnotes

1 Cf. KEVIN CULLIGAN, *The Dark Night and Depression* in *Carmelite Prayer. A Tradition for the 21st Century*, ed. Keith J. Egan (Paulist Press, New York/Mahwah, N.J., 2003), p.119-138.

2 *Spiritual Canticle*, Stanza 1. There are two major

translations in English of the Complete Works. The older is E. ALLISON PEERS, *The Complete Works of St. John of the Cross*, (Burns & Oates, London, 1954). The more recent is KIERAN KAVANAUGH and OTILIO RODRIGUEZ, *The Collected Works of St. John of the Cross*, (ICS Publications, Washington DC, 1979). There are also a number of translations of parts of the Compete Works and particularly of the poetry. This quote comes from ROY CAMPBELL, *Poems of St. John of the Cross*, (Collins, Fount Paperbacks, 1979), p. 15.

3 You may be interested in a fuller development of the stories about the Prophet Elijah in JOSEPH CHALMERS, *The Sound of Silence. Listening to the Word of God with Elijah the Prophet*, (St. Albert's Press, Faversham, UK, and Edizioni Carmelitane, Rome, 2007). This book was first written in Italian: *Il Suono del Silenzio: Pregando con Il Profeta Elia*, (Edizioni Messaggero Padova, 2006).

4 For a development of this idea, see JOHN WELCH, *Seasons of the Heart, A Spiritual Dynamic of the Carmelite Life*, (Carmelite Spiritual Directory Project, Carmelite Communications, Melbourne, Australia, 2001).

5 See JOHN WELCH, *When Gods Die*, (Paulist Press, New York/Mahwah, N.J., 1990).

6 See KEITH EGAN, ed., *Carmelite Prayer. A Tradition for the 21st Century*, (Paulist Press, New York/Mahwah, N.J., 2003).

7 For a brief description of contemplation from the Carmelite perspective, see JOSEPH CHALMERS, *Mary the Contemplative*, (Edizioni Carmelitane, 2001), p. 53-67.

8 *Interior Castle*, I, 2, 8.

9 Mk. 1, 36 in the New *American Bible*, (Thomas Nelson Inc., NJ, USA, 1971). The translation by NICHOLAS KING, *The New Testament*, (Kevin Mayhew, Suffolk, GB, 2004), has *"went chasing after him"*.

10 On the issue of the false self see, ELIZABETH SMITH & JOSEPH

CHALMERS, *A Deeper Love*, (Continuum, 1999). This book is an introduction to the method of centering prayer, pioneered by Thomas Keating in his many books, especially, *Open Mind, Open Heart. The Contemplative Dimension of the Gospel*, (Element Books, USA, 1991).

11 For more detail on the call of Peter, see KLEMENS STOCK, *The Call of the Disciple*, (Edizioni Carmelitane, Rome, 2006).

CONTEMPLATION AND THE CARMELITE RULE

Introduction

Does the Carmelite Rule teach contemplation? My approach will be to try to understand this issue from the standpoint of our spiritual lives today but first we must briefly mention some history. The "Formula vitae", written by St. Albert of Jerusalem between 1206-1214, is in the form of a letter and it is based on the "propositum", or proposal of the hermits on Mount Carmel.[1] It is rather like what happens in our day when an Order asks for a letter from the Pope for some major event. Normally the Order will make a proposal, sending some suggestions on which the Pope might base his letter. Of course the Pope is completely free to reject the proposal and write something completely different. However, presumably in a normal case, the papal letter will be based on the proposal received from the Order.

We know that St. Albert based what he wrote on the proposal received from the hermits, because he tells us so: *It is to me, however, that you have come for a rule of life in keeping with your avowed purpose* (Rule, 3). We can make guesses about what was in the proposal and what comes rather from Albert's own experience but we cannot be sure exactly where each idea comes from. Unfortunately we do not possess a copy of the "formula vitae" written by St. Albert. Kees Waaijman, in his book, *The Mystical Space of Carmel*, which is a Commentary on the Carmelite Rule[2], argues convincingly that the text of Albert's "formula vitae" has been accurately preserved by Felip Ribot († c. 1391) in his collection of documents entitled, *The Ten Books on the Way of Life and Great Deeds of the Carmelites*[3]. The earliest text of the Rule we possess is from the papal bull, "Quae Conditoris" of Innocent IV in 1247. Actually the original of the papal bull is lost though there are several copies in circulation. A copy of the original has been preserved in the Vatican Archives. Pope Innocent gave this bull in response to a request from the Carmelites to adapt the "Formula Vitae" so that they might have a bit more flexibility in regard to their way of life. It is possible to discern what was written by St. Albert and what was added by the Pope. However, the only text of the Carmelite Rule that exists is that of 1247. With the bull, the "Formula Vitae" becomes an official Rule, recognised by the Church and the Carmelite lay hermits became consecrated religious.

Thrust of the Rule

The "Formula Vitae", as is well known, was written at the request of hermits to give official structure to their lives. Pope Innocent IV made some small but significant additions to allow the hermits to become consecrated religious and open foundations in the new cities springing up in Europe. These changes profoundly affected the course that the Carmelite Order would take but they did not profoundly alter its spirituality. The men seeking God in the silence of the cave and in community, listening to the Word of God, and celebrating the Eucharist together, would do so from then on mostly in a new setting. The majority of the brothers would live in the midst of the city but they brought Mount Carmel with them wherever they went. These changes of course did not take place without some internal problems, as is evident from the Ignea Sagitta of the Prior General, Nicholas the Gaul in the 13th century. The Prior General deplores a situation in which Carmelites have left Mount Carmel and flung themselves headlong into active apostolates in cities without adequate preparation.[4]

The present Constitutions of the O.Carm cloistered nuns state,

> *Since its arrival in Europe in the 13th century, the Order had some women united to its spirit in a particular way and who soon committed their lives with the same religious vows as the men of the Order were then doing. The papal document 'Cum Nulla' of Nicholas V (1452), while it approved a situation already in existence, laid the basis for an orderly development of the feminine branch of Carmel so that the 'Blessed Mother of God might be venerated by the women religious, as she was by the men of the Order*[5].

From small beginnings there has arisen a worldwide movement of women dedicated to the service of God and their neighbour by living joyful lives of prayer and penance. This way of life has produced many saintly women, most of whom remain unknown except to God. However, the most famous member of the cloistered Carmelite movement is the great St. Teresa of Jesus, who took the traditional elements and with great ingenuity reworked them for her many foundations. Living in an age of great ferment and upheaval, she incorporated the best of the past in a fresh and creative vision of the contemplative life, a vision, which now influences all Carmelite nuns. Indeed all Carmelite women and men look to St. Teresa as an unparalleled source of inspiration and guide for the spiritual life. In the Constitutions of the O.Carm nuns, the words of St. Teresa are used to express the call, which they have received from God,

> *we feel ourselves 'called to prayer and contemplation. This call explains our origin; we are the descendents of men who felt this call, of those holy fathers on Mount Carmel who in such great solitude and contempt for the world sought this treasure, this precious pearl of contemplation.*[6]

This bears witness that the spirituality of the Order, though the majority of its members at the time were involved in active apostolic works, was still essentially contemplative.

The Order has always considered that contemplation lies at the heart of our vocation. The Institutio Primorum Monachorum, from the late 14th century, which for hundreds of years was the formation document for all young Carmelites, say this:

> *The goal of this life is twofold: One part… is to offer God a heart that is holy and pure from actual stain of sin… The other goal of this life is granted to us as the free gift of God; … to taste somewhat in the heart and to experience in the mind the power of the divine presence and the sweetness of heavenly glory.*[7]

The tradition of the Order has always interpreted the Rule and the founding charism as expressions of the contemplative dimension of life, and the great spiritual teachers of the Carmelite Family have always returned to this contemplative vocation.

Transformation in Christ

The guiding principle of the Carmelite Rule is transformation in Christ. The process of transformation is a gradual growth of the human person in the image and likeness of God and is a constant factor in the mystical tradition.[8] By allowing the values of the Rule to form our lives, we will be gradually transformed so that we become a new creation in Christ. There are many ways of incarnating the Rule. There are still hermits who live it, friars, enclosed nuns, active sisters and very many lay people. All Carmelites are fundamentally called to the same vocation, although they must live it in very different ways.

Christ made very clear what were the conditions of following him. Those who wish to follow him must lose their lives so that they might save them. Our human ways of thinking, loving and acting, which are limited, must be transformed into divine ways, which are infinite. In other words, the Christian vocation is to become like Christ, the image of the invisible God.

The words "contemplation" or "contemplative prayer" do not appear in the Rule. Instead other terms appear like, *"pondering (or meditating on) the Lord's law day and night"* (10); *"your breast fortified by holy meditations"* (19); *"The sword of the spirit, the word of God, must abound in your mouths and hearts"* (19); *"The Apostle would have us keep silence, for in silence he tells us to work. As the Prophet also makes known to us: Silence is the way to foster justice. Elsewhere he says: Your strength will lie in silence and hope"* (21); *"employ every care in keeping silent which is the way to foster justice"* (21). All of these are directed towards transformation in Christ.

Lectio divina

The way of prayer, which is not so much taught but assumed in the Carmelite Rule and which permeates the whole of it, is Lectio Divina. This way of prayer was practiced for hundreds of years before any attempt was made to define it. It was intended to move towards contemplation. It was the way of prayer that had been used by the early monks for centuries before Guigo II the

Carthusian, wrote in the 12th century of the famous four stages or phases of Lectio Divina (reading, meditation, prayer and contemplation).[7] With the rise of scholasticism and the tendency to divide and examine each element in isolation from the others, the natural flow of Lectio Divina towards contemplation became stuck in the area of discursive meditation. All sorts of methods of meditation were laboriously worked out and contemplation tended to be reserved for an elite group within the Church. It was generally thought to be out of reach of ordinary people and indeed dangerous for them. This tendency was reinforced by various movements that arose rejecting the sacramental, hierarchical, institutional Church for a nebulous individual illumination, which exempted individuals even from basic Christian morality. Despite this anti-contemplative milieu, great mystical writers flourished at different periods – e.g. Mechtilde of Magdeburg & Meister Eckhart (13th century), John Tauler, Henry Suso, Ruysbroek and the anonymous English author of the Cloud of Unknowing (14th century) and John and Teresa (16th century).

At the time of the writing of the Rule, there was not much concern about defining stages of prayer. Guigo's four steps of reading, meditation, prayer and contemplation were intended as teaching aids for young people who joined monastic communities; they were never intended to be hard and fast definitions. Lectio Divina was the normal way of prayer for monks and hermits and it was intended to lead to transformation in Christ. That is the point of all authentic ways of prayer or indeed of any Rule. By living faithfully the values of the Rule, we are gradually being transformed in Christ to become what God has created us to be.

The Rule does not teach contemplative prayer; no one can teach contemplative prayer. Lectio Divina forms the background of prayer in the Rule. It was never just a way of prayer; it was and is a way of life. The four phases of Lectio Divina - reading, meditation, prayer and contemplation - flow in and out of each other and form a seamless whole. The hermits did not have four separate times during which they read the Scriptures, meditated on them, prayed about them and then contemplated. They read the Word of God while alone in their cells and while together for meals and for the celebration of the Eucharist or for the recitation of the psalms. Those who could not read, recited the Our Father, of course a Scriptural prayer. They meditated on the Word of God, murmuring the words over and over in their cells or at work outside until the Word became part of them. This led spontaneously to prayer arising from the heart as a response to the Word that they heard. The response could be thanksgiving, repentance, praise or whatever. Contemplative moments could emerge at any point during the day when God took over and the hermits let go of their own words, their own thoughts, their own emotions.

Meditation at this time had nothing to do with discursive thinking about God and the things of God; instead it was a practice whereby the whole body became involved in the prayer. The hermits would murmur the words of the psalms, or even shout them out (hence the need for separate caves on Mt. Carmel). The hermits repeated them over and over until such times as the words took root within them and these words would come spontaneously to mind during their daily work. Clearly St. Albert had meditated long on the Word of God because the Rule is full of Scriptural allusions and direct quotes. The Word of God is part of him and so becomes the heart of the Rule which he wrote. It was the heart of the life that the hermits felt called to follow and which they proposed to Albert.

Our way of praying is different from that of those first hermits because our life is different but the goal is the same. The concept of contemplation has been deeply affected by the history of spirituality. The word "contemplatio" is the Latin rendering of the Greek "theoria", which is an attempt to translate the Hebrew "da'ath", referring to a loving knowledge of God. The word "contemplation" in the strict sense does not appear in the Scriptures but if we understand contemplation as the search for union with God, then clearly the whole Bible is focused on this – the human and divine relationship. Pope Gregory the Great summed up the teaching of the preceding six Christian centuries by emphasising the role of love and knowledge in the work of contemplation. According to Gregory the Great,

> *The fundamental preparation for contemplation, of course, is the devout living of the Christian life through the power*

> *of the Holy Spirit expressed in the virtues of faith, hope and charity and the increasing activity of the sevenfold gift.*[10]

The supreme value of Christianity is not contemplation but love. Contemplation is not an end in itself; it is a means to arrive at union with God. Contemplation is not the reward for great virtue or much time spent in prayer but is that which makes us capable of great virtue, of great love. However the readiness to encounter God immediately and directly in contemplation normally presupposes perseverance at some discursive prayer for a considerable length of time.

As a result of various historical factors, contemplation came to be looked upon with grave suspicion. We know the difficulties, which both St. John of the Cross and St. Teresa had with the Inquisition because of the general suspicion that surrounded contemplation. This suspicion lasted for about 400 years and some of the effects are still with us. One of the most grave effects was that contemplation was cut off from the vast majority of the Christian people and was reserved for an elite group. There was no teaching or preaching about the goal of Christian prayer and most people had never heard of contemplation. This has been partly remedied in recent years with the upsurge of interest in prayer and a rediscovery of the great contemplative tradition within Christianity.

The Catechism of the Catholic Church understands prayer as primarily a relationship with God and only secondly as a specific activity.[11]

The Catechism describes contemplation in the following ways:

> *Contemplative prayer is the prayer of the child of God, of the forgiven sinner who agrees to welcome the love by which he is loved and who wants to respond to it by loving even more. But he knows that the love he is returning is poured out by the Spirit in his heart, for everything is grace from God. Contemplative prayer is the poor and humble surrender to the loving will of the Father in ever deeper union with his beloved Son.*
>
> *Contemplative prayer is the simplest expression of the mystery of prayer. It is a gift, a grace; it can be accepted only in humility and poverty. Contemplative prayer is a covenant relationship established by God within our hearts. Contemplative prayer is a communion in which the Holy Trinity conforms man, the image of God, "to his likeness." Contemplative prayer is silence, the "symbol of the world to come" or "silent love." Words in this kind of prayer are not speeches; they are like kindling that feeds the fire of love. In this silence, unbearable to the "outer" man, the Father speaks to us his incarnate Word, who suffered, died, and rose; in this silence the Spirit of adoption enables us to share in the prayer of Jesus.*[12]

Contemplation is the irruption of God in the human soul. It is a silent, imageless and loving communion with God that transcends all discursiveness. According to St. John of the Cross,

> *Contemplation is none other than a secret, peaceful and loving infusion of God, which if the soul allows it to happen, enflames it in the spirit of love.*[13]

> *Secret contemplation .. is a science of love… which is an infused loving knowledge that both illuminates and enamours the soul, elevating it step by step unto God its Creator.*[14]

It is clear that contemplation is infused, i.e. it comes from God and cannot be grasped by us.

> *So delicate is this interior refreshment that ordinarily if one desires it or tries to experience it, it will not be experienced; because, as I say, it does its work when the soul is most at rest and most free from care; it is like the air which, if one desires to close one's hand upon it, escapes.*[15]

Contemplation is a kind of being to being conversation with no intermediary and no possibility of misunderstanding the communication. In contemplation, God does not come through the senses or through the normal pattern of knowing. God comes from an unknown way infusing directly into our being a loving knowledge of God.

The goal of our prayer is the same as that of the first hermits on Mount Carmel. We seek to pray unceasingly:

> *Each one of you is to stay in his own cell or nearby, pondering the Lord's law day and night and keeping watch at his prayers unless attending to some other duty. (Rule 10).*

We seek to live in the presence of God, to be so in tune with God that everything we do or say or think is according to the will of God. The Rule puts it this way,

> *The sword of the spirit, the word of God, must abound in your mouths and hearts. Let all you do have the Lord's word for accompaniment (Rule 19).*

In this way we are gradually being transformed in Christ.

The path of prayer

St. John of the Cross wrote, commenting on the process of Lectio Divina, that we seek in reading and we find in meditation; we knock in prayer and it is opened to us in contemplation.[16] The first three elements are active – what we can do – and the last, contemplation, is passive – what God does. Contemplation is not confined to a specific time of prayer. According to John, contemplation begins with the dark night of sense,[17] which is not at all an elevated state. Contemplation then begins when we take the spiritual journey seriously and with our whole heart try to respond to God's invitation to intimacy. This necessarily involves us in withdrawing from certain other good things. This withdrawal can cause darkness within us. If we are faithful at this time, God then draws us further and begins to take over the process of transforming us in Christ. At the beginning stages we are still very active, avoiding sin, doing good works, saying our prayers and so on but as the relationship with God develops into a firm friendship, we depend less on ourselves and trust more in God. We have very many lessons to learn on this journey and many ways of acting to unlearn. There are many potholes on this road and also many interesting deviations from the straight and narrow path. It is not always easy to stay on the path that leads to life, especially when darkness falls. St. John of the Cross teaches very clearly that this is a way of faith, which means to trust in God even when the purely human reasons for trust are taken away from us.

As we are growing in intimacy with God, our prayer begins to change. There is a subtle and gradual movement from our effort to God's work. Of course God is at work in any authentic prayer but as we grow in intimacy with God so God gradually begins to take over the steering wheel. The driver obviously determines where the car goes. If we try to interfere with the driving, we will crash. It is important to determine who is going to drive the car. If we simply let go of the steering wheel and God does not take over, we will also crash. At this point, we must take into account the famous three signs of John of the Cross. These are signs pointing to when a person ought to let go of the steering wheel and let God take over, and so give up discursive meditation and pass on to the state of contemplation. The first sign is the realisation that one cannot make discursive meditation nor receive satisfaction from it as before. Dryness is the outcome of trying to fix the senses upon subjects that formerly gave satisfaction. The second sign is an awareness of a disinclination to fix the imagination upon particular objects, exterior or interior. The third and surest sign is that a person likes to remain alone in loving awareness of God, without particular considerations in interior peace and quiet and repose and without the acts and exercises (at least discursive, those in which one progresses from point to point) of the intellect, memory and will.[18] There must be a positive sign that one is being called to contemplation, i.e. the presence of God, and not merely a negative sign of inability to meditate. Therefore one must not anticipate the call to contemplation or drag one's heels when one is called. These three signs in *The Ascent of Mount Carmel* refer strictly to what happens in prayer while in the book of the Dark Night, the three signs are given from another perspective, that of the whole mystical life of which prayer is only a part[19] If the dryness that a person is experiencing comes from God's action, it is not only prayer that changes but the whole of that individual's life.

Those three signs are written with a particular understanding of discursive meditation, which of course was very different from the type of meditation practiced by the hermits on Mount Carmel. I doubt whether many people actually use discursive meditation any more. However, I think that the term "meditation" in John's understanding includes any kind of prayer where we remain active in some sense. After active prayer, no matter how gentle this activity may be, comes contemplation, which is a secret, peaceful and loving inflow of God into the soul.[20] Contemplation is the work of God, not ours. God determines when and if it happens, not us. We can and must prepare ourselves in every way for the gift of God, when and if God wishes to give it to us.

Because of the suspicion that was cast on contemplation and which remained in the Church for several centuries, most people were actively discouraged from any kind of silent prayer. St. Teresa in the "Way of Perfection" showed how one could become a great contemplative by reciting the Our Father[21]. God cannot be defeated by human regulations.

Listening to God

The medieval mind was rather different to ours. Our modern mind is always thinking things out, planning for the future, dwelling on the past. Our minds do not stop; we have an internal tape or cd that accompanies us throughout the day with incessant noise. We are either commenting on this or reacting to that. Often our prayer is simply part of this incessant noise and is not truly an opening of our whole being to the Living God. We want to follow our own agenda instead of responding to the gentle invitation of God to enter into the intimate life of the Blessed Trinity. The central point of Christianity is that we are called into an intimate relationship with God in and through Jesus Christ. In this relationship we are transformed and become what God knows we can be - like God, able to see creation with the eyes of God and love creation with God's heart.

For any successful human relationship, we must take time simply to be with the other and listen deeply to the other. However, we are not very good at really listening. We hear what we want to hear; we filter what is said to us through the sieve of our own agenda. We have difficulty hearing the other because of the constant noise inside ourselves. If we do this in daily life, we do it also at the time of prayer. Part of the transformation process is that our human and therefore limited ways of thinking and loving must be transformed into divine ways.[22] When we read or meditate or even when we speak spontaneously to God, we are in control and it is very difficult for us to let go so that God can take over. St. John of the Cross wrote that God spoke one word and that word was His Son; this Word God repeats in an eternal silence and in silence must it ever be heard by the soul.[23] Lectio Divina moves towards silence, and this silence is the best way of receiving the gift of contemplation. When our words and our beautiful thoughts are no longer sufficient, only silence can give an adequate response to the Word of God and only with an interior silence can we listen to God.

For Carmelites, silence is a very important virtue. From our Rule, we know that silence is the way to foster justice or holiness. (Rule 21). Words and actions that do not come from a silent heart are bound to lead to injustice and simply add to the problems of the world and not to their solution. By silence I do not mean when we are not talking because we are watching television. We must have a solid practice of daily prayer in which silence is an important element. Lectio divina is a practice hallowed by many centuries of use. In this method, there is a time to read, a time to meditate on what we have read, a time to respond to what we have read and then a time when we put down the Bible and let go even of our own holy words and thoughts when we allow the Word of God to take hold of our hearts. What is false within us hates silence because the silence puts the spotlight on it and so there will always be the temptation to fill the silence with words or thoughts, anything at all will do as long as it distracts us from this terrible silence!

Silence is the ambience in which contemplation flourishes. As John of the Cross wrote

> *What we need most in order to make progress is to be silent before this great God with our appetites and our tongue, for the language He best hears is silent love.*[24]

The mere absence of thoughts, emotions, activity or distractions does not constitute prayer of any kind. As Thomas Merton wrote,

> *An emptiness that is deliberately cultivated, for the sake of fulfilling a personal spiritual ambition, is not empty at all: it is full of itself. It is so full that the light of God cannot get into it anywhere.*[25]

However progress in prayer is often characterised by the gradual transformation of many words and thoughts into the simplicity of loving surrender.

We need to learn how to become silent. The first fruit of authentic prayer is self-knowledge, which always remains an essential part of a healthy spiritual life.[26] We cannot come to know God without learning a great deal about ourselves and often this is very painful. When we learn some painful facts about ourselves, we must try to do something about them. Our prayer will not go well if we refuse to give up some sin.

> *No matter how high your contemplation may be, seek always to begin and end your prayer with the knowledge of yourselves.*[27]

Intimate Friendship

A Christian contemplative is a mature friend of Jesus Christ. One who has been through various ups and down and who is now established in a firm and profound relationship with him. It is not static - very far from it - it is always moving and developing. When we come to this point, then our lives become really fruitful because they now are according to the mind and heart of God. We see with God's eyes and love with God's heart.

Contemplation is God's gift. We cannot demand to become God's intimate friends. No friendship can be forced. God is completely sovereign but we know from the Scriptures that God invites us into the life of the Trinity. Many of the Fathers of the Church stressed that God became one of us so that we might become God. No more profound vocation could be given to us.

Contemplation is not some esoteric experience of bliss. It is a process of maturing. The process of contemplation changes the human ways of thinking, loving and acting into divine ways. Our human ways are very limited and so when we read the Word of God, we are limited by our experience of life and by many other factors. It is said that one can find in the Bible reasons to support any position. An example of this is the huge number of little churches all claiming the Bible as their source. It is therefore not sufficient just to read the Bible; our way of looking at things must be purified. When we meditate on the Word of God, we try to understand its meaning and what message it may have for our lives but when we do this, we are still limited. Our little world must be enlarged and our minds reformed according to the mind of Christ. When we pray from the heart, we are still using human words. Our words and thoughts, no matter how beautiful, are still human words and thoughts and it is therefore necessary that they too be purified by the Word of God. The light of God's Word shines a powerful light into the dark corners of our heart. It is very difficult to accept what becomes clear in the light but if we do, we can be set free to become what God knows we can be.

At times prayer can become boring and we can be tempted to give it up. The reason for our boredom at prayer could be personal sin, lukewarmness or an inability to listen. However, it might also be a call from God to move on to another way of relating. This is where we move from friendliness into friendship. There are normally various crises before we become firmly established in a true friendship. We know from St. Teresa that God sometimes treats His friends in a strange way.

The dark night, a concept connected forever with the name of St. John of the Cross is a moment of transition into an intimate and lasting friendship and it can go on for many years. The experience is different for everyone because each relationship is unique. Fundamentally what the dark night experience is all about is that we are invited to leave a way of relating to God where we were in control and move into a new land where God leads us. The dark night is a very normal experience that takes place both in prayer and in daily life. Our meditations and our holy thoughts can only take us so far; at some point we have to let go and trust God to take us further. If our experience of meditation had always been profound and full of devotion, we would never give it up. So God will dry up this source in order to feed us in another way but because we are not used to this other way, we begin to complain bitterly. Reading the Bible at this time is like reading the telephone book. Our profound thoughts on the mysteries of the faith are a distant memory. We cannot raise a single holy thought or holy feeling. Often we also come across various difficulties in our ministry or home life.

The journey of transformation is normally long with many twists and turns, as all that is false within us is gradually transformed into Christ. The dark night is a great blessing from God. It is the time when God is reaching into the hidden places of our hearts in order to transform us completely. The dark night is not dark at all. On the contrary, it is very bright, too bright for us and so it seems to be dark.

This is a crucial time on the spiritual journey. Many give up and turn back because they do not understand what is going on. If we are really trying our best, despite our many sins, and are faithful to prayer, it is very likely that all this darkness is a result of God's action, to lead us out of spiritual immaturity towards becoming His mature friends. There is a great revolution, which takes place in the spiritual life when we finally discover and accept that God is not part of our world but we are part of God's world.

It is critical at this time just to wait on God and to listen for the sound of God's voice which often comes to us in very surprising ways and by means of very surprising people. Albert wrote his "formula vitae" to the hermits who lived beside the spring. This is the spring of the prophet Elijah and the hermits must have been aware of his great example. In the stories in the books of the Kings we see Elijah experiencing great success, then failure. He makes his journey through the desert to Mount Horeb, the mountain of God to rekindle his faith. There he encounters God not in any expected way but in the sound of sheer silence. We too have to be prepared to receive God as God wishes to approach us and therefore we must develop a listening heart.

In contemplation our normal ways of knowing and understanding are stilled and at first there can be the feeling of anxiety that we are doing nothing. So contemplation is a strange new land where everything natural to us seems to be turned upside down, where we learn a new language, the language of silence. We learn a new way of being, not to be always doing but simply to be, where our thoughts and concepts, our imagination, senses and feelings are abandoned for faith in what is unseen and unfelt, where God's seeming absence to our senses is God's presence and God's silence to our ordinary perception is God's speech. It is entering into the unknown, letting go of everything familiar we would cling to for security. Entering this new land at first is like entering darkness and emptiness. It is entering into a process, which is a kind of death but this is the death that Jesus tells us leads to life.[28]

Contemplation begins when we entrust ourselves to God, in whatever way God chooses to approach us. Prayer is the door to contemplation and without prayer we cannot hope to lead any kind of spiritual life. I am convinced, however, that contemplation is much more than prayer but the heart of the matter is prayer. It is a process of transformation, which leads the human being to become a new creation by being transformed in God.

The testing

We do not start the spiritual journey as already transformed. We are marked by our fallen nature and so there is a selfish part of us no matter how holy we may feel or may appear to others. St. John of the Cross points out the many faults of the beginner in his book, "The Dark Night" so that he or she will realise that perfection is still a long way off. We can be totally focused on the fulfilment of our own selfish needs and desires, without really being aware of this. It is vital to understand that we do not become holy simply because we begin to take God seriously. The selfish part of us is quite happy when we take religion seriously so long as it can use its new surroundings to fulfil its own desires.

We will be tested often and the reason for this testing is that we need to be purified so that we will be able to serve others from a pure heart. However, we do not begin the journey with a pure heart; it is a gradual process. Therefore very often our prayer will be dry but that does not mean that God is not talking to us. God normally speaks outside the time of prayer in the midst of our daily life. The contemplative process is much wider than the time we give to prayer but we cannot claim to be contemplatives unless spending time alone with God is an important part of our lives. It is during this time that God gradually purifies our spiritual senses so that we will be able to discern God's voice in the midst of the many other voices we hear each day. Sometimes God speaks words of consolation to us but sometimes God will point out to us something that needs to be changed. It is vital that we accept this and do something about it otherwise we will not grow. Of course the selfishness within us will use all sorts of arguments for not changing and these will sound very reasonable.

The human heart is very subtle and requires a profound purification. This is the purpose of the contemplative journey. As we grow more and more in the likeness of Christ, we learn to see ourselves as we really are. To be a contemplative means to have penetrated the mystery of God by loving knowledge. This is the gift of God and the result of God's purifying and transforming action within the human being.

The call to contemplation is not for the faint hearted; it is not for those who seek spiritual experiences. Contemplation leads to death, the death of all that is false within us, which is in fact a liberation but which must be experienced as death first of all. Thomas Merton described contemplation in the following terms:

> *If we set out into this darkness, we have to meet these inexorable forces. We will have to face fears and doubts. We will have to call into question the whole structure of our spiritual life. We will have to make a new evaluation of our motives for belief, for love, for self-commitment to the invisible God. At this moment precisely all spiritual light is darkened, all values lose their shape and reality, and we remain so to speak, suspended in the void.*[29]

As God reveals to us the hidden motivation of our hearts, we discover that our faith, hope and love are in need of radical purification. Our reasons for believing, hoping and loving seem no longer to be valid, or at least no longer sufficient. At the beginning we will have given ourselves to God as we perceive God to be. We will build up a structure for our spiritual lives, a structure with which we feel comfortable and which supports our image of who God is and what it means to lead a spiritual life. At a certain point this structure will begin to shake because it is in fact built on sand. It seems that if we seriously desire to stand in the truth, our faith, hope and love must be utterly purified. God may seem to disappear and leave us in a more profound darkness than we have ever experienced before. We cannot turn away from God even though we may feel that God has turned away from us. We cannot go backwards and yet we cannot seem to go forwards.

The reason for this experience, I would hazard to suggest, is that there is no point in replacing one set of human reasons for faith, hope and love with another set no matter how deep these latter may be. The only valid foundation for surrendering oneself into the hands of the Invisible God is simply that God is. In God's time the darkness will reveal itself as God's presence.

The contemplative path is not a series of sublime spiritual experiences but involves the stripping of all that is false so that one stands in the Truth. At times this may involve anguish and doubt but there is nothing in heaven or on earth that can compare to the gift of God, which is given to those who truly consent to God's presence and action. The contemplative path is a process of dying and rising. Without the death of the false self there can be no resurrection. The resurrection is pure gift; there is nothing the human being can do to earn it. We can only wait

Contemplation and the Carmelite Rule

in the darkness trusting that it is God's good pleasure to give us the Kingdom (Lk. 12,32).

The acid test of progress on the spiritual journey is whether we are becoming better human beings. How we actually treat other people is the testing ground of the authenticity of the transformation, which is taking place within us. We cannot make progress in the life of prayer unless we progress in the love of God and a very practical love of neighbour.[30] Teresa sought to make progress in the love of God and neighbour. She wrote

> *when I see people very diligently trying to discover what kind of prayer they are experiencing and so completely wrapped up in their prayers that they seem afraid to stir, or indulge in a moment's thought, lest they should lose the slightest degree of the tenderness and devotion which they had been feeling, I realise how little they understand of the road to the attainment of union. They think that the whole thing consists in this. But no, sisters, no; what the Lord desires is works.*[31]

John says in one of his maxims,

> *He that loves not his neighbour abhors God.*[32]

Transformation is not just a change of one or two externals; it is a profound change of what motivates us in daily life. Our motivation is often hidden from us but it determines how we act and react throughout the day. It is this motivation that has to be purified at some point on our journey. Our external behaviour may be angelic or it may be a crucifixion to ourselves and/or to others but we really cannot change very much until such times as we have changed the root cause. Changing external behaviour is often necessary but no change will last unless the underlying motive is also changed. The latter is much more difficult.

Conclusion

The Carmelite Rule does not teach contemplative prayer; it prepares the way for it. The Rule provides the elements of a spiritually healthy way of life that leads people towards transformation in Christ. The Rule, as we have said, assumes the rhythm of Lectio Divina, which leads towards contemplation. We can decide to read the Word of God and to ponder on it. Our response to the Word is usually spontaneous and the fruit of what has gone before but nevertheless we are still in control. Contemplative prayer happens to us. We have no control when it comes to contemplative prayer. This is God's action and we are put to sleep in a sense while God, the great Physician, operates deep within us to transform those hidden recesses of our hearts into the image of Christ. The process of contemplation goes on in daily life but reaches a high point in contemplative prayer. At the beginning contemplation is so vague and so gentle that the individual will normally be unaware that anything unusual is taking place. In a few people this awareness grows enormously and we can see the results of this contemplative awareness in the abundance of mystical literature throughout the centuries. We are very fortunate in Carmel to have several men and women who have received the gift of contemplation as well as the gift of being able to describe their experience for the benefit of others.

Contemplation is a pure gift of God. Like salvation, it cannot be merited. God is not an idol whom we can control by means of the right ritual. We cannot force God to grant us the gift of contemplation, in the final stages of which, we are united with God in a way that words cannot express and our understanding cannot grasp:

> *Eye has not seen, nor has ear heard, nor has the human heart conceived, what God has prepared for those who love Him.*[33]

Endnotes

1 See K. WAAIJMAN, *The Mystical Space of Carmel*, (Peeters, Leuven, 2001).
2 Ibid., p. 17-19.
3 *The Ten Books on the Way of Life and Great Deeds of the Carmelites*, Richard. Copsey, (trans and ed, St. Albert's Press, Faversham, and Edizioni Carmelitane, Rome, 2005).
4 See Critical edition in A. STARING, *Nicolai Prioris Generalis Carmelitarum Ignea Sagitta* in Carmelus, 9, 1962, p.237-307.
5 Constitution 19, quoting a letter of Bl. John Soreth, Prior General, Oct. 14th, 1453.
6 ST. TERESA OF JESUS, *The Interior Castle*, V, 1, 3, cited in Constitution 61.
7 Bk. I, chap. 2. See the recent English translation of this work, R. COPSEY, (trans and ed) *The Ten Books on the Way of Life and*

Great Deeds of the Carmelites, by F. Ribot, c. 1385 (St. Albert's Press, Faversham, and Edizione Carmelitane, Rome, 2005).

8 H. BLOMMESTIJN & K. WAAIJMAN, "L'Homme Spirituel a L'Image de Dieu Selon Jean de la Croix", in *Juan de la Cruz, Espritu de Llama*, Vacare Deo X, Studies in Spirituality Supp. I, (Institutum Carmelitanum, Rome, & Kok Pharos Publishing House, Netherlands), p.623-625.

9 *The Ladder of the Monks and the Twelve Meditations*, (London, Mowbray, 1978).

10 B. MCGINN, *The Growth of Mysticism, The Presence of God*: A History of Western Christian Mysticism Series (SCM Press, London, 1994), p.56.

11 *Catechism of the Catholic Church*, (Geoffrey Chapman, London, 1994) Art. 2558.

12 Ibid. 2712, 2713, 2717.

13 JOHN OF THE CROSS, *Dark Night*, I,10,6.

14 Ibid, 2,18,5.

15 Ibid. I,9,6.

16 *Maxims on Love*, 79.

17 e.g. *Ascent* II, 6, 8.

18 *Ascent*, II,13,2-4.

19 *Dark Night*, I, 9.

20 Ibid I,10, 6.

21 *Way of Perfection* 25,1.

22 Cf. *Constitution* 17 of the *Carmelite Constitutions*, Carmelite Communications, Australia, 1996.

23 *Maxims*, 21.

24 *Maxims*, 53.

25 T. MERTON, *Contemplative Prayer*, (Image Books, Doubleday, New York, 1990), p. 94.

26 TERESA OF JESUS, *Interior Castle*, I,2,8-9.

27 JOHN OF THE CROSS, *Spiritual Canticle*, 39,5.

28 Mt. 10,39.

29 T. MERTON, *Contemplative Prayer*, p. 77.
30 Cf. TERESA OF JESUS, *Way of Perfection*, 4.
31 *Interior Castle*, 5,3,11.
32 JOHN OF THE CROSS, *Other Maxims*, 8 or Otros Avisos, 183.
33 I Cor. 2,9-10.

THE GOD OF OUR CONTEMPLATION

Who is this God who has called us and whom we seek to serve? Many barbarous deeds have been done in the name of God throughout history and in our present day. Sometimes religious piety has been used to hide the lust for power and to provide a sense of security in a changing world. As we grow and mature, our image of God changes because no image we can have of God is God. We are challenged to examine our image of God by the secularism of our times and the rise of the otherworldly sects in many parts of the developing world. Carmelites speak much of contemplation, which is the transforming action of God within us, but who is the God of our contemplation?

The Carmelite Charism

The Carmelite charism speaks of a deep human hunger for God. A charism is a gift given by God to an individual or a group for the benefit of the Church and the world. In the case of our Order, we of course have no founder, in the strict sense of the term, to whom we look back; we have our foundation in a group of hermits who gathered on Mount Carmel. We do not know much about these men or even when they went to Mount Carmel. It is likely that they went to the Holy Land at the time of the Crusades and perhaps some of them were soldiers. However between 1206-14, these hermits had formed themselves into a sufficiently cohesive group that they wished to seek the approval of the Church for themselves as a community. They had made a proposal regarding their way of life and based on this, St. Albert, the Patriarch of Jerusalem, wrote to them a letter containing a series of principles on which their life together should be based. They had no need of the weapons of the Crusaders; instead they were to take up spiritual weapons in the spiritual combat (Rule, 18-19).

After some difficulties, finally Pope Innocent IV definitively approved the Carmelites in 1247, and the letter of St. Albert became an officially accepted religious Rule within the Church. The Pope made some modifications to adapt the Rule to cover friars who were engaged in an active apostolate in the new cities. However these changes had profound implications for the Order because our forefathers thus joined the mendicant movement and identified with the new urban poor and sought to serve them. The Rule of St. Albert contains within it in a nutshell all the fundamental principles of the Carmelite charism. The hermits are named as those who live near the spring. This was the spring named in honour of Elijah the prophet. The fact that they also lived on Mount Carmel made it inevitable that they would have a devotion to the Prophet as all hermits looked to him as their model. St. Albert laid down:

> *An oratory should be built as conveniently as possible among the cells, where, if it can be done without difficulty, you are to gather each morning to hear Mass. (Rule, 14).*

This oratory was named in honour of Our Lady and this is the beginning of the special relationship between Carmelites and Mary, their Mother, Sister and Patroness.

The fundamental thrust of the Christian, and therefore the Carmelite life, according to the Rule of St. Albert, is to live in allegiance to Jesus Christ. The rest of the Rule works out the way in which Carmelites are to follow Christ. St. Albert uses the idea of the armour of God (Eph. 6, 10-17) to instruct the hermits. This concept would have been particularly relevant in time of war and great uncertainty. Carmelites are to put on the breastplate of justice (Rule, 19) and later, silence is declared to be the way to foster justice (Rule, 21). The values of prayer, fraternity and prophetic service are particularly important for us. The Word of God is central to our way of life. Like Our Blessed Lady, we are to ponder on this Word, and it will transform our lives. Indeed the guiding principle of the Carmelite Rule is transformation in Christ. By allowing the values of the Rule to shape our lives, we will gradually be transformed and become a new creation in Christ.

The way of prayer, which is not so much taught but assumed in the Carmelite Rule and which permeates the whole of it, is Lectio Divina. This way of prayer was practiced for hundreds of years before any attempt was made to define it. The famous four stages or phases of Lectio Divina (reading, meditation, prayer and contemplation) come to us from Guigo the Carthusian about the year 1150 in his book, "The Ladder of the Monks". At the time of the writing of the Rule, there was not much concern about defining stages of prayer. Guigo's four steps of reading, meditation, prayer and contemplation were intended as teaching aids for young people who joined religious communities; they were never intended to be hard and fast definitions. Lectio Divina was the normal way of prayer and it was intended to lead to transformation in Christ. Meditation at this time had nothing to do with discursive thinking about God and the things of God; instead it was a practice whereby the whole body became involved in the prayer. The hermits would murmur the words of the psalms and repeat them over and over until such times as the words took root within them and they would come spontaneously to mind during their daily work. Clearly St. Albert, and the hermits, had meditated long on the Word of God because the Rule is full of Scriptural allusions and direct quotes. The Word of God was part of their lives and so became the heart of the Rule which he wrote.

The Rule provides the elements of a spiritually healthy way of life that leads people towards transformation in Christ. The Rule does not teach contemplative prayer; it prepares the way for it. Despite the fact that the words "contemplation" and "contemplative prayer" are not mentioned in the Rule, other terms are used that point to this reality for example: "pondering (or meditating on) the Lord's law day and night" (10); "your breast fortified by holy meditations" (19); "The sword of the spirit, the word of God, must abound in your mouths and hearts. And whatever you do, let it all be done in the Word of the Lord." (19). The Rule, as we have said, assumes the rhythm of Lectio Divina, which leads towards contemplation. We can decide to read the Word of God and to ponder on it. Our response to the Word is usually spontaneous and the fruit of what has gone before but nevertheless we are still in control. Contemplative prayer is qualitatively different from any other prayer that has preceded it. We lose our control when it comes to contemplative prayer. This is God's transforming action within us and we are put to sleep in a sense while God, the great Physician, operates deep within us to transform the hidden recesses of our hearts into the image of Christ. Of course this is not completely passive as the Song of Songs declares: "*I slept but my heart kept vigil*" (Sg. 5,2). The process of contemplation goes on in daily life but reaches a high point in contemplative prayer. It cannot be grasped; it can only be received:

> *So delicate is this interior refreshment that ordinarily if one desires it or tries to experience it, it will not be experienced; because, as I say, it does its work when the soul is most at rest and most free from care; it is like the air which, if one desires to close one's hand upon it, escapes.*[1]

At the beginning, contemplation is so vague and so gentle that the individual will normally be unaware that anything unusual is taking place. In some people this awareness grows enormously and we can see the results of this contemplative awareness in the abundance of mystical literature throughout the centuries.

Contemplation

The Order has always considered that contemplation lies at the heart of our vocation. The *Institutio Primorum Monachorum*, which from the late 14th century was the formation document for all young Carmelites, states that the goal of the life is to offer God a heart that is holy and pure from actual stain of sin and the other goal is a free gift of God, which is to taste *"the power of the divine presence and the sweetness of heavenly glory"*.[2] St. Teresa and St. John of the Cross were well formed in the Carmelite tradition and recalled the Order to its initial inspiration, as did all the other reforms throughout the history of the Order. Saints Teresa and John of the Cross of course are original spiritual geniuses and for those who wish to understand more of the development of contemplation within the individual, study of these saints is essential.

In the current presentation of the Carmelite charism, the Order says the following in the Constitutions of the friars:

> *Carmelites seek to live their allegiance to Jesus Christ through a commitment to seek the face of the living God (the contemplative dimension of life), through fraternity, and through service in the midst of the people (Const. 14).*

Another article of the Constitutions of the friars goes on to say

> *The tradition of the Order has always interpreted the Rule and the founding charism as expressions of the contemplative dimension of life, and the great spiritual teachers of the Carmelite Family have always returned to this contemplative vocation. (Const.17).*

According to the Constitutions of the friars, contemplation

> *is a transforming experience of the overpowering love of God. This love empties us of our limited and imperfect human ways of thinking, loving, and behaving, transforming them into divine ways. (Const.17).*

In the Constitutions of the affiliated Congregations and the recently approved Third Order Rule, there appears the same insistence on contemplation.

The *Ratio Institutionis Vitae Carmelitanae* (formation document hereinafter referred to as the Ratio) of the friars clarifies the role of contemplation in the charism of the Order:

> *The contemplative dimension is not merely one of the elements of our charism (prayer, fraternity and service): it is the dynamic element which unifies them all.*

> *In prayer we open ourselves to God, who, by his action, gradually transforms us through all the great and small events of our lives. This process of transformation enables us to enter into and sustain authentic fraternal relationships; it makes us willing to serve, capable of compassion and of solidarity, and gives us the ability to bring before the Father the aspirations, the anguish, the hopes and the cries of the people.*
>
> *Fraternity is the testing ground of the authenticity of the transformation which is taking place within us. (Ratio 23).*

The Ratio goes on to say

> *Through this gradual and continuous transformation in Christ, which is accomplished within us by the Spirit, God draws us to himself on an inner journey which takes us from the dispersive fringes of life to the inner core of our being, where he dwells and where he unites us with himself.*
>
> *The inner process which leads to the development of the contemplative dimension helps us to acquire an attitude of openness to God's presence in life, teaches us to see the world with God's eyes, and inspires us to seek, recognise, love and serve God in those around us. (Ratio 24).*

The goal of the contemplative journey is to become mature friends of Jesus Christ to such a degree that his values become our values and we begin to see with God's eyes and love with God's heart. Authentic contemplation must find expression in a commitment to serve others, whether this is done by means of an active apostolate or within a monastery. When God gazes on the world, God sees beyond the externals; God sees the motivation of the human heart. A contemplative community's authentic experience of God necessarily leads us to make our own

> *the mission of Jesus, who was sent to proclaim the Good News of the Kingdom of God and to bring about the total liberation of humanity from all sin and oppression. (Ratio, 38).*

To see with God's eyes

In the post-synodal document Vita Consacrata, Pope John Paul II wrote

> *At the beginning of his ministry, in the synagogue at Nazareth, Jesus announces that the Spirit has consecrated him to preach good news to the poor, to proclaim release to captives, to give sight back to the blind, to set the oppressed free, to decree a year of favour from the Lord (cf. Lk. 4,16-19). Taking up the Lord's mission as her own the Church proclaims the Gospel to every man and woman committing herself to their integral salvation. But with special attention, in a true preferential option, she turns to those who are in situations of greater weakness, and therefore in greater need. 'The poor', in varied states of affliction, are the oppressed, those on the margins of society, the elderly, the sick, the young, any and all who are considered and treated as 'the least'. The option for the poor is inherent in the very structure of love lived in Christ. All of Christ's disciples are therefore held to this option, but those who wish to follow the Lord more closely, imitating his attitudes, cannot but feel involved in a very special way. The sincerity of their response to Christ's love will lead them to live a life of*

> *poverty and to embrace the cause of the poor. For each institute, according to its charism, this involves adopting a simple and austere way of life, both as individuals and as a community. Strengthened by this living witness and in ways consistent with their choice of life, and maintaining their independence vis-à-vis political ideologies, consecrated persons will be able to denounce the injustices committed against so many sons and daughters of God, and commit themselves to the promotion of justice in the society where they work. (VC, 82).*

Faithful to the Scriptures, the Church and the Order have made a preferential option for the poor because Christ was sent to bring Good News to the poor. (Lk. 4,18). We cannot remain untouched by the cry of the poor. (cf. Ex 22,22.26; Sir. 21,5). A commitment to Justice and Peace necessarily involves doing something concrete for the poor but it also involves asking questions. Why is the situation like this? What can we do about it? Obviously the reasons for the situation of poverty of so many in the world and the reasons for the lack of true peace are extremely complex. This preferential option comes from our contemplative vocation.

> *The authentic contemplative journey allows us to discover our own frailty, our weakness, our poverty - in a word, the nothingness of human nature: all is grace. Through this experience, we grow in solidarity with those who live in situations of deprivation and injustice. As we allow ourselves to be challenged by the poor and by the oppressed, we are gradually transformed, and we begin to see the world with God's eyes and*

> *to love the world with his heart. With God, we hear the cry of the poor, and we strive to share the Divine solicitude, concern, and compassion for the poorest and the least.*
>
> *This moves us to speak out prophetically in the face of the excesses of individualism and subjectivism which we see in today's mentality - in the face of the many forms of injustice and oppression of individuals and of peoples. (Ratio 43)*

The fundamental reason for the existence of so much poverty in the world lies in the depths of the human heart. It is a great mistake to blame only others for the situation because each of us bears some responsibility. The commitment to Justice and Peace must go hand in hand with the contemplative process of putting on the mind of Christ so that our service of the poor does not become a subtle way to make the poor serve our own needs. The human heart is very devious, and, in order to serve others according to the mind and heart of God, we must submit to the profound purification, which is an intimate part of the contemplative process. (Jam. 4,8; Heb. 4,12-13).

The Prophet Elijah

In recent years the Carmelite Family has rediscovered the importance of the Prophet Elijah as an inspiration in the work of justice and peace. His contemplative experience impelled him to prophetic action. He denounced without fear the actions of the powerful people of his day and he brought the light of the Word of God into situations of sin. The story of Naboth's vineyard (1 K.21, 1-29) is a good example of Elijah's prophetic activity. King Ahab wanted Naboth's vineyard for himself but Naboth did not want to sell his patrimony. The Queen, Jezebel, mocked her husband and challenged him to show who in fact was King in Israel. The queen had hatched a diabolical plot to accuse Naboth unjustly of blasphemy and to assume the control of the vineyard when Naboth was out of the way. The Prophet Elijah came on to the scene when Ahab had taken the vineyard into his possession and he condemned Ahab for abusing his authority. Obviously this was a very courageous step. Proclaiming the Word of God in certain situations can be very dangerous. In the Prophet Elijah, we see a man who translated his contemplative experience into prophetic action.

Elijah won a great victory for Yahweh on Mount Carmel (1K. 18,36-40) but he was threatened by Jezebel and immediately his internal voices drowned out his trust in God. He went into the desert, (1K. 19,3-4) which is traditionally the place of silence. (Hos. 2,16). God spoke to Elijah through the angel so that Elijah would continue his journey. Elijah had difficulty in discerning the voice of God in the midst of all his troubles but eventually plodded on to Horeb. (1K. 19,5-8) When he arrives, God asks him what he is doing there. Elijah replies that he is filled with great zeal for the Lord God of hosts. He tells God that he is the only champion of Yahweh remaining in the whole of Israel. (1K. 19,10) God does not respond at this point but simply tells Elijah to go out and stand on the mountain. There Elijah meets God but not in the way he expects nor in the way that his whole religious tradition has taught him to expect. Elijah has to silence all his internal voices that tell him what God is like so that he can receive God as God is. (1K. 19,11-12) Once Elijah has met God on God's terms, and not on his own terms, he is open to hear the truth, which sets him free from illusion. He thought that God really needed him since he was the only prophet left. God very gently points out that in fact there are 7000 others who have not bent the knee to Baal. (1K. 19,18) Now freed from illusion, Elijah receives a new mission from God, which is in fact mostly carried out by his successor, Elisha, who is the recipient of a double portion of his spirit. (1K. 19,19; 2K. 2,11)

God uses everything, big or small, good or bad, to challenge our normal way of being in the world, just as Elijah was challenged to let go of his expectations of how God would come to him. These expectations were deeply rooted in Elijah and our expectations and perspectives are deeply implanted in us. Before we can receive God as God really is, we have to learn to let go of all these. This is a painful process, a real dark night, but essential so that we can bear the light of day and be prepared for the encounter with God. Our Carmelite tradition speaks of a journey of transformation. The events of our life are not meaningless. At the heart of every event, God is calling to us to take a step forward on our journey. God is calling to us to take a step forward from our predictable way of judging situations and people, including ourselves, so that we can begin to see things from God's perspective. The end of our journey is our completed transformation when we are able to look upon all that is as if with God's eyes and love what we see as if with God's heart. We need to eat and drink lest the journey be too long for us. We find the necessary food for our journey in the daily celebration of the Eucharist, pondering the Word of God and in our Carmelite tradition.

Mary the Mother of God

Carmel is famous for its Marian devotion, which is expressed in many ways. The greatest devotion is to be conformed to the object of our devotion. Titus Brandsma said that the vocation of a Carmelite was to be another Mary. The "fiat" of Mary gave the necessary space for Christ to be born and thus she co-operated with the plan of God. Through her, God now has a human face. Our devotion to Mary must not stop at the imitation of her virtues, though that is very important. We must allow Christ to grow within us to the point that we become transformed in him so that we can say with St. Paul, "it is no longer I who live but Christ who lives in me". (Gal. 2,20) In that way we will be a word from God, a tabernacle of the presence of God in the world. (cf. 1Cor. 3,16; Eph. 2,21-22) In that way we will live our prophetic vocation.

The divine maternity was the subject of much reflection among the Carmelites from the earliest

The God of our Contemplation

times. As an Order with a strong contemplative thrust, the Carmelites sought to gaze on God even here on earth. Our Lady was the model of all they were aiming to be. No closer union with God could be thought of than Our Lady carrying God's only Son in her womb. The fact that she was sinless meant that there was no resistance in her to God. Her faith made her unswerving in her trust in God no matter what happened. She listened attentively to the Word of God and did what God asked of her. In this way she came to the fullness of life.

Mary had to walk by faith. She had to penetrate the mystery of God's plan and the mystery of her Son with loving faith. She pondered everything that happened to her and stored up everything in her heart in order to follow where God desired to lead her. (Lk. 2,19.51). All the disparate elements of life reveal something of God and of God's plan. Mary is presented to us as a model. (Lk. 11,28). She is the woman of faith, the perfect disciple of Jesus Christ. By imitating her faith, we are enabled to see beyond the external things that surround us. She was able to "see" God at the heart of the universe drawing all things and all people to Himself through Jesus Christ. Mary was a contemplative, which does not mean that she spent all day on her knees. A contemplative is a mature friend of God who looks upon reality as if with the eyes of God and loves what she sees as if with God's heart. Prayer of course is very important but the test of the authenticity of prayer is how we live in daily life. Even prayer can be used as an escape from reality. The reality that surrounds us is the place of the encounter with the Living God. This reality can be difficult; it can be challenging but nevertheless it is the sacred space where we meet God. Prayer is not just bombarding God with requests and petitions; it is above all an opening of our hearts, our lives, to God. God has a plan for us and for our world and this plan is borne out of love for us. God does not impose on us but invites us to be co-workers in making the divine plan a reality in our world. We cannot pray with sincerity "Your Kingdom come" unless we seek to bring the values of the Kingdom to our own little part of the world.

In prayer we invite God into our lives to shape and mould our hearts so that we can be instruments of God's peace and love, so that we can be tabernacles of the divine presence. Jesus himself gave us the model of all prayer. (Mt. 6,9-13; Lk. 11,1-4). God is Father of all and therefore all of us are members of the same family. We bless and thank God because by our faith we have grasped something of the divine plan for us and therefore we desire that God's will may be done. Mary was eager that God's will be accomplished and she was more than willing to play her part. This eagerness for God's will remained unchanged despite the sufferings that came to her because of her acceptance. She proved that her prayer really was an opening to God by her acceptance and active co-operation with God's will.

We are asked to be faithful to God in our own particular situation. We are asked to live the Gospel where we are. We are asked to be contemplatives at the heart of the world, being aware of God's presence not in dramatic ways but in the midst of our ordinary everyday lives. Each of us then will be a focus for God's presence in our own little part of the world. First of all in faith we need to be aware of the presence of God within us and then in the people we meet. God lives at the centre of each human being no matter what that person is like. As we become more and more aware of God's presence everywhere, we become more sensitive to the signs of the presence of God's Kingdom. This appears clearly in the visit of Mary to Elizabeth and in the beautiful words of the Magnificat. (Lk. 1,39-55).

The Hebrew Scriptures speak of watchmen on the towers. They would be the first to see the dawn of a new day from their high positions. (Is 21,11-12; 40,9). The psalms speak of people who get up very early in the morning to anticipate the dawn. (Ps. 57(56),9; 108(107),2-3; 119(118),147-148). We are to be "Kingdom spotters" (people who can recognise the values of the Kingdom in unlikely situations (cf. Lk. 17,20-21; 12,54-56)). Many people with no obvious religious affiliation live by the values of God's Kingdom, the same values that Jesus lived by and taught. (cf Lk. 10,13-14). We will be able to spot these even in the most unlikely people and encourage these values wherever we meet them. The visit of the poor shepherds to the crib and what they said made Our Lady ponder in her heart. (Lk. 2,8-20). She recognised the hand of God at work.

Prophets of Justice and Peace

God is not deaf to the cry of the poor and neither must we be deaf. In the words of the Prophet Isaiah, God says

> *Is not this rather the fast which I desire: break unjust fetters, untie the thongs of the yoke, set free the oppressed and break every yoke? Does it not consist perhaps in sharing your bread with the hungry and to bring the oppressed and homeless into your own home, in clothing those who are naked without neglecting your own people? (Is. 58, 6-7).*

We live in God's world and creation has been entrusted to us as God's stewards. (Gn. 1,28; Sir. 17,1-4; Wis. 9,2-3). This does not mean that we have complete liberty to use or abuse the goods of the earth without thought for tomorrow or for future generations. We have certain rights but also certain duties towards the rest of creation. The Word of God is concerned with the whole of life and not just spiritual things. (Ps 104(103),27-30).

Jesus Christ is for us the primary model of what it means to be a prophet. We are above all followers of Christ and therefore we must seek to put into practice his teachings every day. Jesus Christ is priest, prophet and king because in him all the promises and roles of the Old Testament are fulfilled. He is the one in whom the work of the prophets reaches its culmination. (cf. 2Cor 1,20; Mt 7,12). The prophets of the Old Testament proclaimed the Word of God in particular situations. They warned and condemned but also comforted the people in times of difficulty. They sought to turn the hearts of the people towards God (Mal. 3,24) and they spoke with severity or with tenderness according to the situation.

The prophets of the Old Testament spoke to the imagination. They asked the people to imagine another possible future. For example the prophets Isaiah and Micah spoke in a time of war of a time of peace when

> *from their swords they will forge ploughshares and from their blades, scythes. No nation will lift the sword against another nation and they will not learn the art of war anymore… (Is. 2,4; 11,5-9; Mic. 4,3).*

When the future is very dark, the prophets bring hope. However in order to do this, it is necessary to see beyond the present situation to the reality that lies beneath. This is the faith of Our Lady in the Magnificat who sees the proud cast down, the hungry filled with good things and the rich sent away empty when those who see only the external appearances would believe the opposite to be true. (Lk. 1,46-55).

God has sent us a saviour and in Jesus we see the way that God works in our world. Jesus preached Good News, healed the sick, pardoned sinners and welcomed those who were excluded by the religious leaders of his day. He did not resist violence when it came to him as a result of his fidelity to the Father. He willingly and freely gave up his life on the cross so that we may have life and have it to the full. (Jn. 10,10). He faced the full force of evil and seemed to be submerged by it but the Father raised him to life on the third day. (Heb. 5,7-9). The resurrection of Jesus means that love is stronger than hatred or evil, life is stronger than death. (Rom. 8,35-39).

To be a peacemaker is a Christian obligation. (Lk. 10,5; Mt. 5,9). It is not an optional extra to our Christianity. What does being a peacemaker mean for us? First of all I think that we need to make ourselves aware of the root causes of conflict in our world. We often cut the heads off weeds and they simply grow again. There can be no lasting peace until the causes for discontentment have been addressed. We can go even further back in our search for the root of causes any war or injustice. The name of God is used for many demonic actions. It is the safest mask of Satan and we must continually tear this mask off if we are to be peacemakers. The great spiritual tragedy is that many cruel and inhuman acts are committed in the name of serving God. (Jn. 16,2). Our father Elijah struggled against the worship of idols and indeed the great danger in his day was that the people might claim to worship Yahweh but in fact were worshipping the idol Baal. (1K. 18,16-39). Idol worshipping is still prevalent in our day. The names of the idols may have changed but the substance is the same. An idol is any person, place or thing, that we put in the place of God and from which we seek complete happiness. It is very easy to condemn other people for the evils that they do. It is much more difficult to see and accept the truth that we are part of the evil which we protest against.

Jews, Christians and Muslims venerate the Prophet Elijah and so we Carmelites must be ecumenical in our outreach. This would be a real prophetic action in the situation of our days. We cannot contribute to peace in our world until we are at peace in our own hearts, until we are able to live in peace with the people around us. The lack of peace in our own lives contributes to the lack of peace in our world.

But what can we do? We have no political power. How can we change the world? We can certainly take seriously the suggestions that are presented to us by our local and International Justice and Peace Commissions. The Carmelite Family has recently formed a Carmelite NGO (Non Governmental Organisation), associated to, and recognised by, the UN. That has given us a much wider forum in which to share our charism. There are many Carmelites involved in promoting justice and peace as a constituent part of working for the coming of God's Reign. We need to be aware of the many signs of hope that exist. Who would have thought that they would have seen the tearing down of the Berlin Wall or the dismantling of the Eastern Block? What was responsible for these major events? Obviously there is no simple answer to that question. However can we not say that the thousands of little people who struggled and suffered for justice for many years had some effect? Ordinary people can change things. Take the example of slavery. For a time keeping slaves and making vast sums out of selling some human beings to other human beings was considered to be perfectly socially and morally acceptable. However several people in a number of countries decided to do something about this. Within a few years they had changed the attitude of whole societies.

We can certainly also pray for peace and justice in our world. However in a situation in which the world is threatened by annihilation, prayer does not mean much when we take it only as an attempt to influence God or as a search for a spiritual fallout shelter or as a source of consolation in stress-filled times. Real prayer is such a radical act because it asks us to criticise our whole way of being in the world; lay down our old self and accept our new self, which is Christ.

The sound of sheer silence

Where is God in the midst of all our problems? (Ps. 42(41),4; 79(78),10; Joel 2,17). Our faith tells us that God cannot really be absent from our lives. That would be hell. The Prophet Isaiah speaks of the hidden God. (Is 45,15). Perhaps we need to learn to discern the presence of God in the apparent absence of God and to learn a new language, God's language. St. John of the Cross, tells us that,

> *One word the Father spoke,*
> *which word was His Son,*
> *and this word he speaks*
> *ever in eternal silence,*
> *and in silence must it*
> *be heard by the soul*[3].

We have to cultivate a profound silence within so that we can hear what God wants to say to us. (cf. Is 50,4). We need to listen to God in prayer of course but also in the events of daily life. Often we have so much noise going on inside us that we cannot hear or discern anything else. As Carmelites, this silence should come naturally to us, or at least the desire for it. This is not just an ascetic practice and it is not referring merely to an external silence. It is an internal silence in order to discern the presence of God in the midst of even the most hopeless situation so that we can continue our journey with hope. Our Rule tells us:

> *The apostle recommends silence, when he tells us to work in it. As the prophet also testifies, Silence is the cultivation of justice; and again, in silence and hope will be your strength.(Rule 21)*

We need to try to identify the noise inside us: the commentaries on others, on events, and on ourselves. Once we have become aware of our internal noise, we can begin to let it go so that it does not influence everything we do, think and say. If we continue the journey we will be brought face to face with our prejudices, our irrational fears and our presumptions. This experience is not to depress us but so that we can be liberated from them.

It is necessary to cultivate an interior silence so that we will be aware that God is speaking to us through some simple and humble messenger. If we are not silent within, life passes us by and we never grasp the true significance of what happens to us.

(cf. Mt. 16,1-3). Many of us are not completely at ease with external silence. We have an internal tape or cd that comments on everything and everyone throughout the day. The comments on the internal tape are based on our particular perspective on life, which of course is usually in our favour. We instinctively defend ourselves if we feel under attack and we seek the esteem and acceptance of others. We do this usually without being aware of what is going on inside us. It is a constant internal noise that makes it difficult to hear any other voice. The journey of faith towards transformation takes us through bright sunlight and dark valleys. (cf. Ps 23(22),4). God uses all the events of our life, good and bad, as instruments of purification, which is essential if we are to become what God has created us to be. We have to make the effort to attempt to discern the hand of God at work but this discernment is much easier if we can calm the noise inside us and hear the voice of God who speaks in the sound of the gentle breeze, or as some exegetes have it, "the sound of thin silence" or "the sound of sheer silence" (I K 19, 12).

Say no to death

We àre the people of the resurrection. The resurrection is God's "yes" to life. If we are to say "yes" to life, we must say "no" to death in all its forms. Saying "no" to death starts much earlier than saying "no" to any form of physical violence. It requires a deep commitment to the words of Jesus -

"Do not judge". (Lk. 6,37). It requires saying "no" to all violence of heart and mind. (Mt. 5,22). The judgements I make of people are a form of moral killing. (Rm. 14,4). When I judge other human beings, I label them, put them in fixed categories and place them at a safe distance from me so that I do not have to enter into a real human relationship with them. By my judgements I divide my world into those who are good and those who are evil and I thus play God. But everyone who plays God ends up by acting like the devil. The words of Jesus go right to the heart of our struggle, *"Love your enemies, and do good to those who hate you. Bless those who curse you. Pray for those who treat you badly."* (Lk. 6,27-28).

What my enemy deserves is not my anger, rejection, resentment or disdain but my love. (Mt. 5,44-45). Only a loving heart, a heart that continues to affirm life at all times, can say "no" to death without being corrupted by it. Increasing starvation and poverty around the world, the wars that go on all the time offer us many reasons to be fearful even despairing. When we hear the voices of death all around us and see the many signs of the superiority of the powers of death, it becomes hard to believe that life is indeed stronger than death. However, it must have been hard to believe in a bright future on the first Good Friday.

Our God is a God of surprises. If we say "no" to death in all it forms, we may seem to be on the losing side. Indeed at times it may seem that we are on our own but we are not. There is a whole army of unimportant people, in the eyes of the world, praying and working for peace. These people are allowing God to change their lives from within, to take out of their bodies the heart of stone and replace it with a heart of flesh, which is able to love. (Ez. 11,19). These people are letting go of the false self which is based on external criteria e.g. success, wealth, power, the good opinion of others and so on, and discovering the true self which is found in God. The true self is created in the image and likeness of God. (Gn. 1,26-27) and nothing can destroy it. The true self does not judge others or label them but it sees another true self struggling to release itself from the chains of the false self. This army of peaceful people is having an effect on our world. Jesus said, "Blessed are the meek for they shall inherit the earth". (Mt. 5,5). The power of our God is stronger than all human weapons. (Jud. 9,7; Is. 40,15). When will the promise be fulfilled? We do not know but fulfilled it will be.

Jesus Christ is the Word of God (Jn. 1,14), God's "yes" to the world. God created the world and found everything very good (Gen.1,31). Through creation we can come into contact with God (Rm. 1,20) and therefore we have a serious duty to protect it and nurture it so that it will continue to speak of God to future generations. By means of the death and resurrection of Christ we are redeemed and reunited with God. (Rm. 6,4-11). The Word of God does not return to its author without having completed what it was sent to do, according to the prophet Isaiah. (Is 55,11). This is true in a sublime way in the case of Jesus Christ through whom the whole of creation finds once again the road that leads to God. (John 14,6).

To become a word from God it is necessary to enter a process of interior transformation and consent to the presence and action of God in our life. This is the work of God but God will not do it without our consent. This process can be painful because through it we come to see ourselves as we really are and not as we would like to be. The great danger is that we will seek to run away from this encounter with ourselves because we do not want to accept what is being revealed to us. This process of transformation includes a disintegration of what is false within us so that the true self can come to birth.

We do not fulfil our prophetic vocation simply by preaching or when we work with the poor and the marginalised, vital though that work is. We fulfil our prophetic vocation when we become a word from God and this involves a death in view of a resurrection, a new life in the image of God. To work for justice is an essential element of the preaching of the Gospel. This has been underlined innumerable times in church documents. However those who work in the area of justice and peace often meet with incomprehension or even antagonism from their own brothers or sisters. Why is not easy to explain but this fact has obscured a very important element of our work as religious.

A Dark Night

In our faith journey, there are moments when we are brought into the desert. Sometimes we walk into the desert following God's call or sometimes we just find ourselves there by force of circumstance. The desert is arid and it can be a frightening place. What does it all mean? We can be tempted not to go any further on the journey because we feel it is just not worth all the trouble. Then God sends a messenger to us. (cf. 1K. 19,4-7). This messenger can come in all shapes and sizes and he or she encourages us to eat and drink for the journey is long. We are encouraged to eat the bread of life and drink from Carmel's wells, that is the Carmelite tradition, which has given life to many generations before us. But perhaps we are too depressed to even be aware of this, so God's messenger nudges us again and encourages us to eat and drink. It is a great challenge to recognise what God is saying to us in the midst of daily life and to recognise the voice of God in and through the voice of some very unlikely person.

Our faith, hope and love, those three essential Christian virtues, are at the beginning of our journey, based on what we have learned from others. As we continue on the journey, our human reasons for belief, for hoping in God and for loving as Christ commanded, begin to fail us. They are no longer sufficient. We can throw it all in because the journey is too precarious and the end is uncertain or we can reject the messenger and stay right where we are. Or we can continue the journey into the night. (1K. 19,4-7). An essential element on our journey towards transformation is the dark night. This was never intended to be gloomy and impossible but an invitation to let go of our human and limited way of thinking, loving and acting so that we can think, love and act according to God's ways.[4]

John of the Cross gives masterful descriptions of various elements that go to make up the night but it is not uniform for everyone. The night is experienced by each person in a different way and is made precisely to assist the purification of the particular individual. The dark night is not a punishment for sin or infidelity but is a sign of the nearness of God. The dark night is God's work and leads to the complete liberation of the human person. For this reason it is to be welcomed despite the pain and confusion involved. The dark night can be experienced not only by individuals but also by groups and whole societies. (cf. Lam. 3,1-24).

The journey of transformation usually lasts a long time because the purification and change that is wrought in the human being is so profound. This is not just a change of idea or opinion; it is a complete transformation of how we relate to the world around us, to other people and to God. The Native American Indians have a saying about walking a mile in someone else's moccasins before we can understand another person. Jesus warned his followers not to judge (Lk. 6,37; Rom 14,3-4) and the reason is very simple: we cannot see things from another person's perspective and therefore we do not know what are the motives behind his or her actions. The process of Christian transformation, however, leads the human being towards a profound change of perspective, from his or her own particular way of seeing things to God's way. This involves a profound purification and emptying of all our attachments so that we can be filled with God.

This contemplative journey, both on a personal and communitarian level, cleanses our hearts that we may truly have room in our hearts for others and may have the possibility of hearing the cry of the poor without translating it through the filter of our own needs. We will then be able to carry out the challenge laid down by Pope John Paul II:

> *Consecrated men and women are sent forth to proclaim, by the witness of their lives, the value of Christian fraternity and the transforming power of the Good News, which makes it possible to see all people as sons and daughters of God, and inspires a self-giving love towards everyone, especially the least of our brothers and sisters.*[5]

Our Response

Our vocation as Carmelites is very profound. We are called to serve the people as contemplative communities. By responding to Christ's call to follow him, we pledge ourselves to take on his vision and values but we soon find that we are incapable of living up to our ideals on our own. As we mature in our relationship with God, we give space to God to purify us so that we begin to see the way God sees and love as God loves. This way of seeing and loving is painful for the human being because it requires a radical transformation of the heart. The cry of the poor will penetrate our defences and our response, freed from the distortion of the false self, will be from a pure heart.

Commitment to justice, peace and the safeguarding of creation is not an option. It is an urgent challenge, to which contemplative and prophetic Carmelite communities, following the example of Elijah and of Mary, must respond, speaking out in explicit defence of the truth and of the divine plan for humanity and for creation as a whole. Our community lifestyle is in itself such a statement: it is founded on just and peaceful relations, according to the plan outlined in our Rule. In St. Matthew's Gospel, Jesus reminds us: *I assure you, as often as you did it for one of the least of my brothers and sisters, you did it for me."(Mt. 25, 40).*

Endnotes

1 *Dark Night*, I, 9,6.
2 Bk. I, chap. 2. See the recent English translation of this work, R. COPSEY, (trans and ed) *The Ten Books on the Way of Life and Great Deeds of the Carmelites*, by F. Ribot, c. 1385 (St. Albert's Press, Faversham, and Edizione Carmelitane, Rome, 2005).
3 *Maxims & Counsels*, 21.
4 cf. *Constitutions of the Friars*, 17.
5 *Vita Consecrata*, 51.

ST. THÉRÈSE OF LISIEUX
FOR THE THIRD MILLENIUM

Introduction

In recent years St. Thérèse of Lisieux has been much in the news. In 1997 the centenary of her death was celebrated.[1] During this year there was the solemn proclamation that she was henceforth to be considered as a Doctor of the Church and therefore numbered among the saints whose teaching is put forward as particularly profound and helpful.[2] Her relics have been carried to many countries and everywhere the sceptics have been confounded. Many more people than anyone imagined would be the case have welcomed the visit of the relics.

All these events give cause for celebrating the life of this great saint but also give us the opportunity to re-evaluate her message in the light of the questions of present day men and women. What relevance has St. Thérèse of Lisieux to our global situation in the first few years of the third millennium? How can she help us to follow Christ in our world that has seen so many changes and where the pace of change is increasing every day? She herself seemed to have lived a very narrow life. Her family was like a little oasis of intense Catholicism in the middle of a French culture, which was rather antagonistic to traditional Christian faith. Her sisters undertook most of her education at home and her venture into a normal school was not a great success. She followed two of her sisters into the strictly enclosed Carmelite monastery of Lisieux at the age of fifteen, contrary to the advice of several wise people. She lived her Carmelite vocation quietly until her early death at the age of twenty-four. She became widely known and very popular after her death due to the publication and extensive dissemination of her autobiographical writings that had been heavily edited by her well meaning sisters.

Her popularity spread very quickly and her "Little Way" was recognised and practiced by many as a profound spiritual discipline. She was canonised in 1925 and declared "Patroness of the Missions" by Pope Pius XI in 1927. There was huge support from all over the world given to the proposal for her to be named "Doctor of the Church". It is unusual to come across a Catholic church anywhere in the world that does not have a statue of St. Thérèse. There is quite a leap from the obscurity of an enclosed life to such heights of fame. Ever since her death St. Thérèse has exercised a powerful influence on millions of people throughout the world who have found in her "Little Way" a sure guide for their everyday lives. However many others found her image as "The Little Flower" to be saccharine and a great obstacle to being able to hear her message. Unfortunately the image of Thérèse and her writings were the object of pious editing in order to make her fit the accepted ideas of sanctity of the times. God of course does not always fit in with our accepted ideas and since we have been able to read what Thérèse actually wrote there has been a re-appraisal of this saint and her importance for our age.

The contemplative vocation of St. Thérèse

First of all, what is meant by "contemplative vocation"? Many people on hearing that term would immediately think of a woman who feels called to live a life dedicated to prayer in an enclosed monastery. Indeed most people would immediately think of the kind of life that Thérèse in fact followed in the Carmel of Lisieux. However that kind of life is very specialised and most Christians are not called to live in that way. Reducing the contemplative vocation to a particular state in life would be to greatly impoverish the term and to exclude the vast majority of the Church from this call.

Much of the writings of the past on contemplation were couched in a language that is not easily accessible to most people. However there exists an immensely rich contemplative tradition within Christianity and the great figures of this tradition describe in manifold ways the call to an intimate life of union with God. For a number of reasons, suspicion was cast on the contemplative call but fortunately it was not completely extinguished but contemplation came to be understood as only for an elite group in the Church. As a result the immensely rich Christian contemplative tradition was hidden from all but the specialist. The 1960's witnessed the rise of a new hunger for an experience of God and many people walked away from the faith in which they had been brought up and were attracted to various Eastern religions that had developed methods of meditation, which held out the possibility of a deeper experience of God. Despite the rise of dogmatic secularism, there exists a similar hunger for spirituality in our own days and some have turned to various New Age remedies to find a way to God. There is a deep hunger in human beings for God. We have been created with a capacity for God and nothing created can fill these "deep caverns of feeling"[3] even though we often try to do so. Only when we are "filled with the utter fullness of God" (Eph. 3,19) can this hunger be satisfied. The profound contemplative tradition within Christianity thankfully in our days is once again being made available to all.[4]

Pope Paul VI believed that our world has greater need of witnesses than teachers.[5] In the writings of St. Thérèse we will not find a lengthy treatise on the nature of contemplation but we do find an outstanding witness to the transforming power of God's loving mercy. Thérèse opened up the hope to all people of every state or condition, that they too could enter into an intimate relationship with God. She offers hope that life in the end means something. According to the theologian Hans Urs von Balthasar

> *The great saints are surely signs that the Holy Spirit sets up through the course of history to show the Church the*

> right road, both doctrinal and practical, which she would
> have trouble finding and following without them.⁶

Thérèse certainly did not understand herself as a member of an elite. She believed that sanctity was within the reach of all since it simply meant being open to whatever Jesus wants.⁷ I believe that her experience of God opened up the possibility of intimacy with God for all those who desire this with their whole heart and who had never dared think that such was possible for them.

Yet surely an enclosed Carmelite nun is so out with the normal experience of life that she can have little to say to people in general? How few people understand the value and the meaning of the enclosed contemplative life! Even good Catholic parents are often horrified when their daughter wants to become an enclosed nun. "What a waste of a life!" is often heard. But yet the enclosed life shares in the mystery of the hidden life of Christ. He remained hidden in the obscurity of ordinary life in Nazareth for about thirty years. Even during his public ministry, he did not seek to startle people by amazing signs of power although he was tempted to do so. God's ways are not our ways and his thoughts are not our thoughts (Is. 55,8). We are often tempted to look for God in the extraordinary but in fact He comes to us in the very ordinary. We are tempted to think that we can only serve God in extraordinary feats when instead He seeks only our love, which we can show in every moment of our daily lives.

The enclosed contemplative life is ordinary in the extreme and is dedicated to serving God in a completely hidden way. Most of us live very ordinary lives. St Thérèse shows us that the hidden, ordinary life can be more powerful than all the politicians and scientists. The hidden life baffles reason but in the designs of God, it is the most effective apostolate of all. It works from within like yeast in bread. A little bit of yeast does not look like much but it contains great power and it can make the whole loaf rise.

Due to our present limited understanding, we cannot easily grasp the significance of our ordinary lives. Thérèse was very much aware of the communion of saints, that is the unity of all those who belong to Christ. She firmly believed that although ordinary people are not given much importance in this world *"in heaven, we shall not meet with indifferent glances because all the elect will recognise that they owe to each other the graces that merited the crown for them."*[8]

The Little Way of Thérèse is not confined to those who live in convents but it is also entirely suitable for all people no matter what station in life they occupy. It demands no special feats but shows us how to respond lovingly to God's grace, no matter where we may find ourselves. It gets down to essentials and shows all of us how to do the same. Thérèse rediscovered something very simple and profound - that we have a Father in heaven, that He made Himself known to us through His Son Our Lord Jesus Christ, that without Him we can do nothing, that if we trust in Him and rely on Him, we can do everything or rather He will do it within us.

Thérèse as guide

Thérèse's relationship with God went through various phases of development and thus she can be a guide for those who wish to enter into and make headway on the spiritual journey. Her childhood experiences taught her a great deal and during her early years she learned things that were to prove to be fundamental in her life and to her "little way". Because of her experience of being loved within her family, she came to understand the complete gratuitousness of love but also that love called forth a response.[9] We have come from God and we are going to God and the raison-d'être of human life is love. The foundation of Thérèse's way is her understanding of God as Father. Thérèse learned about the love of God the Father not from books but from life. God was like her own father and just as she could trust him utterly so she could trust God completely. Her relationship with her father provided a springboard for her but when she entered Carmel, she was presented with another face of God – the God of justice who has created hell fire for those who disobey the commandments. This concept of God was considered to be perfectly compatible with the fact that God is love. The God of justice, however, tended to obscure the God of love. This approach to God, heavily influenced by the remnants of the Jansenist heresy that continued to cast its shadow in Thérèse's day, tended to lead to scruples. Thérèse, having recovered from a bout of scruples as a little girl[10], would not give into them again. Never again would she give much importance to her weaknesses. She certainly refused to be ruled by them but they did not bother her greatly because they made her realise her utter dependence on God.

Thérèse was one of the few brave ones who have the courage to swim against the tide of human thinking. She lived in a century where God was often viewed as a God of Justice. Many heroic souls offered themselves in place of the sinners. This required great courage and a heroic love for others but perhaps from our viewpoint appears to be mistaken. Thérèse wrote that on thinking about those souls who offered themselves as victims to the Justice of God to deflect and draw down on themselves the punishments in store for the guilty, she herself did not feel attracted to this at all. She instead considered the immense love of God and how this love is so often scorned and despised.

> *Oh my God, is your scorned love to remain in your heart? It seems to me that if you were to find souls offering themselves as victims to be burnt in the fire of your Love, you would quickly consume them; I think that you would be happy not having to suppress the floods of infinite tenderness which are in you.*[11]

When she made her Act of Self-Offering to Merciful Love, it seems that God accepted the offering. Thérèse understood what love meant. Love is stronger than death. The love of God is like a rushing torrent, a burning fire that consumes all who are willing to open their hearts to divine love.

St. Thérèse of Lisieux for the Third Millennium 181

This consuming is not an end but the fulfilment of every human desire – a consummation.

For one to grow in the relationship with God, it is absolutely critical to believe that one is loved by God. If this belief is not firmly in place, one will not find the courage to enter or stay in the silence that is an important part of the preparation to receive the gift of contemplation. At times the silence can feel empty and unless there is faith, mostly not on the level of feelings, that God is somehow present, one would seek to escape the pain of nothingness. Thérèse tells us that during the period of darkness that she went through, she made more acts of faith than throughout the rest of her life.[12]

Thérèse was at the same time afraid and yet totally fearless. Her fear came from her knowledge of what it means to accept totally God's gift of love and yet her lack of fear was due to her boundless confidence in God. Thérèse had great desires to do wonderful things for God. She wanted to convert the whole world; she wanted to be a missionary; she wanted to be a martyr, a priest, everything at the same time. We know how she was tormented by unfulfilled longings until she read chapters twelve and thirteen of the first letter to the Corinthians in which she discovered her vocation to be love in the heart of the Church, her Mother.[13]

Thérèse had an intense desire to love and to do good but at the same time she realised that she did not have the strength even to walk to the foothills of Mount Carmel, never mind ascend to the summit. She considered herself too small to do great things for God but she did not give in to discouragement in the face of a seemingly impossible task. She realised that God had given her these great desires and God would certainly fulfil them. So, in spite of her nothingness, she aspired to be what God wanted her to be – a saint.[14] Thérèse found the lift that would carry her up to Jesus himself and which would dispense her from climbing up the rough ladder of perfection. From reading certain Old Testament passages[15] she came to realise that the lift, which would carry her to perfection, was the arms of the Lord.[16] Thérèse wanted above all to love but she found that she could not. However, she also discovered the solution to the impossibilities that her ambitions to love encountered. God puts the flame of love into the hearts of those who are willing to be consumed.

Thérèse's desire was to be a saint. She knew that she could never be like one of the great saints and so she was perfectly happy to be a "little" saint. In her way of thinking, holiness consisted in consenting to whatever Jesus wanted to do in her, receiving his love when and how he chose to manifest it. She believed that she would receive everything from God.

Thérèse was open to recognise the approach of Christ in everything that happened to her and therefore she valued each opportunity to love him in his very concrete brothers and sisters who crossed her path each day. From the testimonies of those who knew her, Thérèse's love was warm hearted and she treated each person as a gift from God. She did not simply love the Lord in other people, she was aware also that it was Jesus himself who loved through her:

Yes, I feel that when I am being charitable, it is Jesus alone who is acting in me; the more united I am to Him, the more I love all my sisters.[17]

Thérèse's devotion to the child Jesus is well known. Through this devotion she expressed her total availability to the Lord and consented to the presence and action of God in her life. Perhaps her devotion reached greater depths as she was drawn to reflect on the Holy Face of Christ. Constant meditation on the passage from Isaiah, which speaks of the man of sorrows (Is. 55,1-5), led her to a deep love of humility and suffering. A love of suffering sounds very strange to modern ears. We know that Thérèse was opposed to extravagant penances and mortification that were self-imposed because these could easily be subtle forms of self-love. Her goal was not suffering but Christ the Lord who chose the path of suffering during his earthly life.

Perhaps it is in her attraction to suffering and especially in her experience of darkness that we touch the core of what contemplation is. From early on she experienced a desire for suffering and indeed a love for it.[18] Beautiful thoughts and feelings can be merely surface emotions while suffering goes to the very core of one's being. Even prayer can be used as a security blanket; even prayer can be used to avoid the face-to-face encounter with the Living God. There is a kind of person who uses many words but manages to say very little or nothing and often hides behind an unending flow of rhetoric. We can relate similarly to God. Unfortunately there is nothing more devious than the human heart (Jer. 17,9) and so when we use prayer as a security blanket, we are often able to effectively hide this from ourselves. We can also misunderstand experiences in prayer and be led astray by them. Prayer can be subtle self-seeking if we begin to seek nice feelings instead of seeking God alone. Therefore extraordinary experiences in prayer or even simply nice feelings can in fact draw the individual away from the whole point of prayer, which is to be united ever more closely with the Lord. In order to be united, one must be purified of all that is not God. When one truly consents to God's presence and action in one's life, God takes the process of purification to a new level because we are willing to co-operate in this great work. Before we can be purified, we must really accept the need to be purified. It is not enough to have an intellectual knowledge of this; it must be experienced. God will begin to show the person gradually the layers of motivation behind his or her actions. The way of prayer does not bolster what is false within us but shines a light into the darkness and gives God space to dismantle what is false and encourages the growth of the true self. Contemplation is a process of transformation of the human being.

Thérèse suffered in a number of ways but worst of all were her inner trials. When she entered

Carmel, she rarely received consolations in prayer. Thérèse did not become distressed over her seeming lack of progress. She understood prayer as simply

> *a movement of the heart, a simple glance cast towards heaven, a cry of recognition and of love whether the in the midst of difficulties or joys; it is something great and supernatural that expands the heart and unites me with Jesus.*[19]

In the last eighteen months of her life, she was plunged into the deepest, darkest night of faith. Thérèse had been brought up in an intensely Catholic atmosphere. She breathed in faith everywhere and she was protected from harmful outside influences. She responded totally to the God in whom she believed and this in itself would have been enough to make her a great saint. However God has given her to the world as a great saint for our modern times. We live in a post-Christian era and everywhere dearly-held beliefs are questioned or rejected outright. Things that were taken for granted for centuries are now put under the microscope. In the early years of Thérèse's life, heaven was more real than earth. God was the centre of her life. Then in the last eighteen months of her short life, God seemed to have disappeared. Heaven seemed to be a cruel myth. Thérèse's innocent faith gave way to terrible doubts. Death beckoned her not as the gateway to life with God whom she loved with all her heart but as the night of nothingness.[20] To someone like Thérèse for whom faith had been as natural as the air she breathed, this must have been a dreadful suffering. Yet, with the benefit of hindsight, it was inevitable because of her passionate desire for truth.

The call to contemplation

God granted St. Thérèse's desire for truth. God seemed to go missing from her life and leave her completely alone. Everything disappeared for her but the work of love. She began to understand atheists for the first time and she marvelled that there were not more suicides among those who had no faith in God. She ate the bread of sinners and shared the table with the hopeless. She was happy to stay there as long as God wanted it that way.[21]

Thérèse accepted the weakness of her nature and instead of complaining about it, she saw in it an opportunity for a wonderful display of God's mercy. When we allow God to come close to us, we begin to see ourselves as we really are – often proud, jealous, over-sensitive about ourselves and lacking in sensitivity for the feelings of others, lukewarm with regard to God and so on.

In her upbringing, Thérèse came into contact with the Word of God through the pious practices of her family. Even as a young girl, Thérèse began to practice meditation even though she did not realise what she was doing. She thought a great deal about the events that were happening all around her and the beauty of nature led her to reflect deeply. Her first visit to the sea at a very young age led her to ponder on the vastness of God.[22] There were various personal events in her life that deeply affected her and caused her to think very seriously about her life. She pondered on what she saw and on her experiences. This deep thought led her to a deeper awareness of God and of God's will for her.

St. Thérèse abandoned herself into the arms of her loving Father. God accepted this self-abandonment and made her a great saint. Thérèse understood that to be a saint meant to be totally available to the radical demands of love whatever that might entail. However, when God, who is love, begins to make demands of us, we begin to realise our own absolute poverty. All the grand illusions of an earlier period of the spiritual journey begin to crumble. Thérèse realised that she could not accomplish her desires. The mountain was just too high and the paths too steep. She desired to love God more than God had ever been loved. She seized the smallest opportunity to show her love but despite all this she realised that she could not attain her desire. Through her experience of several years of failure to live up to her ideals, she gained a new and vital insight into the spiritual journey. She never lowered her ideals to make them more easily attainable. Instead she learned that it was God's good pleasure to lift her to the top of the mountain. In order for this to happen, she could place no trust in herself but all her trust had to be placed in God. She learned that she could not pile up merits in the sight of God. She would appear before God with empty hands and she had complete confidence that God would fill her hands to overflowing. She would do everything in her power to please Jesus and she believed that he would look after the rest.

Our faith and hope must be placed in God but God is beyond every human concept. The ideas we have of God, no matter how noble they may seem to be, are not God because God is beyond any idea we could have. God's self-revelation comes to us through creation but even from all the wonders of the world, we receive a very limited picture of God. The self-revelation of God continues through the experience of the Chosen People and the final and complete revelation of God comes to us through Jesus Christ. However, in Christ there are inexhaustible treasures and we will never plumb the depths of Christ. As we continue to walk on the spiritual journey we encounter darkness. God takes us further in the darkness, where our faith, hope and love are purified so that we will cling only to God and not to any human ideas no matter how inspiring these may have appeared to be at one time in our lives.[23]

Conclusion

The unbeliever might say that Thérèse sacrificed her life uselessly and yet there are innumerable witnesses in every continent to her spiritual power. Her education was seriously limited and now she is a master of the spiritual life and a Doctor of the Church. She is one of the most well known and popular saints but also perhaps sometimes misunderstood. Some have thought that her Little Way is a way of reducing holiness to the banal. However, there is no lessening of the Gospel demands in St. Thérèse's way. She is reported to have said:

> *People must not think that our `little way' is a restful one, full of sweetness and consolation. It is quite the opposite. To offer oneself as a victim to love is to offer oneself to suffering, because love lives only on sacrifice; so, if one is completely dedicated to loving, one must expect to be sacrificed unreservedly.*[24]

The Little Way of St. Thérèse involves a very deep conversion of heart. The human being seems to tend towards illusion, the illusion of the false self.[25] The false self seeks itself in all things, even in religious matters where it very easily takes on a pious disguise and can act in a very subtle manner. However, the Little Way is the way of truth, recognising one's reality and the absolute necessity of God's saving action. The way of contemplation too is the way of truth because it leads to the death of the false self through a process of transformation and purification, which is the work of God, who leads us forward gradually forming us to become all that we can be.

Thérèse desired to be a saint but her understanding of what that meant changed as the years passed. Certainly her experience of doubt, darkness and suffering changed her. She desired that God's will be accomplished in and through her. God's ways are not our ways and God's thoughts are not our thoughts (Is.55,8) and so God responded to Thérèse's desire in ways that she did not foresee. To be a contemplative does not mean to live a peaceful life full of sublime experiences of prayer but to be completely open to the purifying and transforming action of God in one's life, however God decides to act. Often this may mean that the person has no felt experience of God's presence and that the activity of God is shrouded in darkness. However, God's presence is manifest to others in the way the individual lives daily life.

The popularity of St. Thérèse can be explained by the fact that people intuitively see in her one who was totally open to God and in whom God's merciful love triumphed. She was completely available to God no matter what the cost. This is the attitude of a contemplative. Thérèse never thought of herself as special; she was one of God's little ones. The best devotion is to take seriously the example of the one to whom we are devoted. Those who are devoted to St. Thérèse pay her great honour when they try to do as she did, i.e. give God complete freedom in their lives and do everything in order to please God. In that way they will be intimate friends of God, without necessarily being aware of it, and they will become what God knows they can be. This is the goal of the contemplative journey. St. Thérèse points the way to all who wish to begin this journey and her example encourages them to continue the journey when the night is darkest. Her purified faith allowed her to believe in the light despite the darkness that surrounded her. Those who truly consent to the transforming presence and action of God in their lives will also be led safely through the valley of darkness to where God desires them to be. The contemplative way is the way of abandonment into the arms of a loving God.[26]

In our days, hope is often placed in what will ultimately betray the human heart. Thérèse, by her life, affirms that God alone will not betray us and will respond to our deepest yearnings. In a very simple way she grasped the heart of the matter: God is Love and when we allow this Love to transform us, we will arrive at the ultimate destination of the human journey. What we need is trust in God's love for us no matter what happens and St. Thérèse shows us the way.

Endnotes

1 Cf. C. MACCISE and J. CHALMERS, *Back to the Gospel. The Message of St. Thérèse of Lisieux*, a letter to all Carmelites from the Superiors General of the Order of Discalced Carmelites and the Order of Carmelites in *In obsequio Jesu Christi*, (Edizioni OCD, Rome, 2003), p. 23-48

2 Cf. C. MACCISE and J. CHALMERS, *A Doctor for the Third Millennium*, a letter to all Carmelites from the Superiors General, of the Order of Discalced Carmelites and the Order of Carmelites in *In obsequio Jesu Christi*, Edizioni OCD, Rome, 2003, p. 51-74

3 JOHN OF THE CROSS, *Living Flame of Love*, B, verse 3

4 For an excellent modern attempt to make the contemplative tradition available to all, see the work of Fr.

Thomas Keating OCSO. His book, *Intimacy with God*, (Crossroad, New York, 1994), tells the story of the foundation of Contemplative Outreach, which is a network of faith communities committed to the process of Christian transformation. One of his other books, *Open Mind, Open Heart. The Contemplative Dimension of the Gospel*, Element, Mass., U.S.A., 1992, is the basic handbook for the teaching of Centering Prayer, which is a method of prayer, intended to remove the human obstacles to the reception of the gift of contemplation. For an introduction to the Centering Prayer method and background, see also ELIZABETH SMITH and JOSEPH CHALMERS, *A Deeper Love. An Introduction to Centering Prayer*, (Continuum, UK & U.S.A., 1999)

5 Cf. *Evangelii Nuntiandi*, 41
6 *The Timelessness of Lisieux* in Carmelite Studies, Vol. 1, ed. John Sullivan, ICS Publications, Washington DC, 1980, p. 104
7 Ms A,2v. The text used for this article is: SAINTE THÉRÈSE DE L'ENFANT JESUS ET DE LA SAINTE FACE, *Oeuvres Complètes*, Cerf, DDB, Paris, 1992, p. 72. All translations are my own.
8 *Derniers Entretiens*, Ibid., p.1048
9 Cf. "Oh Jesus, I know that love is only repaid by love and so I sought and I found the way to bring relief to my heart by returning Love for Love", Ms B, 4r Ibid., p. 227
10 See Ms A, 39r, Ibid., p.132
11 Ms A, 84r, Ibid., p. 212
12 Ms C, 7r, Ibid., p. 243
13 Ms B, 3v, Ibid., p.226
14 Ms C, 2v, Ibid., p. 237
15 See especially Prov. 9,4 and Is. 66,12
16 Ms C, 3r, *Oeuvres Complètes*, Cerf, DDB, Paris, 1992, p. 237-238
17 Ms C, 12v, Ibid., p. 251
18 Ms A, 36r, Ibid., p. 127

19 Ms C, 25r and v, Ibid., p. 268
20 Ms C, 6v, Ibid., p. 242-243
21 Cf. Ms C, 6r, Ibid., p.242
22 Ms A, 21v, Ibid., p. 102-103
23 For St. Thérèse's teaching on the purification of faith and hope, see Ms C, 5v, Ibid., p. 241 and for the purification of love, see Ms C, 11v, Ibid, p. 249
24 From the testimony of Sr. Marie of the Trinity at the diocesan process to inquire into the life and virtues of Sr. Thérèse, in, CHRISTOPHER O'MAHONY, *St. Thérèse of Lisieux. By those who knew her*, (Veritas Publications, Dublin, 1975), p. 236
25 For a simple explanation of the false self and its relation to the spiritual life see ELIZABETH SMITH and JOSEPH CHALMERS, *A Deeper Love. An Introduction to Centering Prayer*, (Continuum, UK & U.S.A., 1999), chapter 8.
26 Cf. Ms B, 1v, *Oeuvres Complètes*, Cerf, DDB, Paris, 1992, p. 220-221.

MARY OBEDIENT TO THE WORD

Lk. 8,19 Then his mother and his brothers came to him but were unable to join him because of the crowd.
20 He was told, "Your mother and your brothers are standing outside and they wish to see you."
21 He said to them in reply, "My mother and my brothers are those who hear the word of God and act on it.

In the well known passage from St. Luke's Gospel Jesus stresses the importance not of physical affinity to him, but of the need to "hear the word of God and act upon it". There is another passage in the same vein in Luke's Gospel:

Lk. 11, 27 While he was speaking, a woman from the crowd called out and said to him, "Blessed is the womb that carried you and the breasts at which you nursed."
28 He replied, "Rather, blessed are those who hear the word of God and observe it."

Because of the important role that Mary plays in St. Luke's Gospel, it is inconceivable that either of these passages is a criticism of the Mother of the Lord; rather they point out that she has heard the word of God and acted upon it. Indeed she is put forward as the model of the one who listens and acts.[1]

Before we can act on the word of God we must first of all hear it and this is not at all easy. We have to listen in order to hear. I remember attending a workshop on prayer and at this event was a profoundly deaf man who was rather mischievous. Due to his disability he had developed the skill of lip-reading. One evening we were doing a form of meditation in a group and we were supposed to close our eyes but our friend pretended not to understand. The leader in mock severity shouted to the deaf man, "I said close your eyes". Very quickly he replied, "If I close my eyes I will not be able to hear you!" Of course everyone burst out laughing. However what the deaf man said was true. We do not just listen with our ears; we must use all our senses. We must develop an awareness of what is happening and what is being said in order that it might penetrate within us.

We can see an example of this in the famous scene of the marriage feast at Cana in St. John's Gospel. While it obviously means more than just a local wedding celebration, we must start off with what the text gives us. In the middle of this great feast, a terrible calamity occurs: they run out of wine. However, on a scale of terrible calamities, it hardly is of earth-shattering importance. It would mean acute embarrassment for the family providing the feast and an end to the festivities but not much more. Everybody is involved in enjoying themselves but Mary sees. She becomes aware of the problem and wants to do something to help. She knows that she can do nothing but goes to the one who has the power to solve the problem. She does not plead but simply presents the problem to

Jesus: "they have no wine". His response seems to be a rejection: Jesus said to her, *"Woman, how does your concern affect me? My hour has not yet come."* (Jn.2,4) Jesus is seeking to do the will of his Father and the time has not yet come. Clearly Mary does not take this response as a rebuff or a refusal because she immediately goes to the servers and tells them, *"Do whatever he tells you."* She tells them to do what she does, that is listen to the word of God and put it into practice. Jesus listens to the Father and through his mother naming the need he hears the command to begin his public ministry. The word of the Father is somehow mediated by the circumstances in which Jesus finds himself and especially by the revelation of the simple need which comes to him through the remark of his mother: they have no wine. Therefore Jesus begins his public ministry. The servers in this story also listen and act upon what they have heard. Jesus tells them to fill the six stone water jars, each holding 20 to 30 gallons. Not only is this is an arduous task, it is also crazy but they do it. Their faith and the faith of Mary are rewarded beyond anything they could have imagined. Not only has Jesus given them the best wine, which is obviously a symbol for the new life that he brings, but he has given 120 to 180 gallons of it!

All of this, according to John, was occasioned because Mary was aware. She "listened" with her eyes. So we are called upon to listen to the word of God with all our senses. The word of God can come to us in many different ways. God speaks to us of course through the Bible, the liturgy, and through our own personal prayer but also through the joys and hopes, the sadness and anguish of our world. A contemplative is a person who is able to discern the presence of God in all situations, whether seemingly bad or good. Our Lady recognised that somehow God was present in the relatively trivial fact of there being no more wine for a feast. She perceived that this was an important moment for her Son and so she presented the problem to him and was the immediate cause of his beginning his public ministry.

Alone and together

In the Carmelite Rule there is an interesting movement from the silence of the individual cell to the gathering in common either in the chapel, in the midst of the cells, or in the refectory where the hermits listened to the word of God while eating together. The time together strengthened the hermits to continue the search for God in the silence of the cell. The time alone, focused on prayer, made sure that each hermit added something to the community. I believe that this movement remains important for all of us no matter what our particular way of life may be. Our being with others helps us to be aware of the "joy and hope, grief and anguish"[2] of our world. This experience drives us to seek the face of the living God in whom alone can be found the answer to our profound questions about who we are and why we are here. This personal search strengthens us to return to the market place so that we can help others to become aware of the presence of God in their lives.

There are some fundamental skills that are necessary in order to be able to hear, whether it is through the ears or the eyes or any other sense! We have to pay attention to the other person. When we meet another person, we are meeting a mystery. Remember the experience of the Prophet Elijah in the desert (1 Kgs. 19,3ff). God sent an angel to him so that he would eat and drink and continue his journey. God is forever sending angels. The word "angel" of course means messenger, and God can use anyone as a messenger. It is best to pay attention to the other person in case he or she is bringing you an important message from God. Perhaps of course what you have to say is much more important than anything the other person could possibly want to say. So much of life will just pass you by. If you know that you have the fault of talking too much and not listening to other people, an excellent penance is to try to be quiet and to listen to what another person is saying.

In Carmelite spirituality silence is a very important value. The Carmelite Rule gives directions regarding external silence but this is in order to protect an internal value. It is quite possible to have perfect external silence but to be filled with noise inside. On the contrary, it is possible to be silent within in a noisy atmosphere.

The false self

The Carmelite Rule speaks of the spiritual armour, which the hermits are to wear (Rule 18-19). They have a battle to fight, not so much against the enemy outside, but the enemy within. It is this interior enemy that makes it so difficult to listen to the Word of God and therefore it must be defeated. The enemy within has been called many things. I want to call it "the false self", which is the selfishness within that is ever ready to invade every aspect of us. Our Lady is the Immaculate Conception. She is without sin, the first of the redeemed. Sin is fundamentally a refusal to listen to God, who tells us that we are loved. Being without sin, Mary had no barriers to God and therefore could hear through every sense, the word that God spoke to her. She was in tune with God and was able to receive without distortion. Our receiving apparatus is not in good shape and therefore does tend to distort everything.

The false self is the human response to the sense of being alone in this big frightening world. We very quickly develop defence strategies to protect us from perceived dangers. We need love; we need security; we need to feel in control. These are all basic human instincts and good but we have been created to be in communion with God and so our desires are infinite in order to be commensurate with the infinite God. Unfortunately we are born into a fallen, though redeemed world. We are subject to the effects of original sin, from which Mary was preserved. One of the effects is that we are born outside of Eden, which is the symbol for union with God. Our hearts really are restless until they rest in God, as St. Augustine said. Therefore our lives are a continual search for shalom, for the Sabbath rest, when all our desires can be fulfilled. Unfortunately we tend to look in the wrong places for the fulfilment of these desires and so we are never at peace.

In order to feed the desperate emptiness within us, we grasp and hold on to what we can. The little baby discovers that adults do its bidding when it cries or smiles and so unconsciously manipulates them. In a baby these little ways are charming but as the child grows, we begin to say that he or she is spoiled. When the child becomes an adult, if he or she has not matured as a human being and still manipulates people, he or she becomes dangerous. If the child is starved of love, security and the sense of control, he will seek after these things as an adult.

People continually seek the symbols of security, of love and control, even when they objectively do not need them. A politician was sent to prison for corruption on a vast scale. He accepted bribes amounting to a huge sum of money. The judge at his trial said to him, "You were not cold. You were not wet. You were not hungry? Why did you do it?" The politician had no answer. He was aware that he had wasted his life. Why did he do it? He had more than enough but even that was not enough. He sought more and more wealth until his whole life collapsed under the weight.

The false self makes it very difficult to hear the word of God. However it is very subtle. When you make the decision to follow Jesus Christ and enter the Carmelite Family, the false self is very supportive. The false self does not care what kind of life you want to live as long as it remains in control. It simply shifts its focus from the symbols of security available in one lifestyle to those available in another. In one kind of life, the symbols of affirmation, security and control might be possessions, for example a big car, a big house and so on. Following Jesus Christ, these things hopefully become much less important, but we have other symbols.

The false self makes a lot of noise. It drowns out anything else with its incessant demands to be catered to. If it feels in any way threatened or that its constant demands are not being met, and they will never be fully met since it is insatiable, it becomes very defensive. The word of God can easily be manipulated to feed the false self, which makes its home in the spiritual life if that is what you want. The armour, of which the Carmelite Rule speaks, is needed because the spiritual journey involves a ferocious battle against the false self. If you do not defeat it, it will take you over and dominate every aspect of your life. It is not sufficient to listen to the word of God; we must also act on it. Remember the story of the two sons (Mt. 21, 28-30) who were both asked by the father to go and work in the vineyard. One said, "yes, of course" but did not go; the other refused but in the end repented and went into the vineyard.

We must seek to quieten the noise within us, which the false self makes with its constant demands to receive signs of esteem, of security and to ensure its own survival. These demands can seem to be absurd to others but perfectly correct to the person under the domination of the false self. We must have a great and very determined determination, as St. Teresa said writing of the commitment to prayer.[3] This determination must be to put the whole of the Gospel into effect and not just the bits that appeal to us. Perhaps a temptation for those committed to justice and peace work might be to forget that, without a serious commitment to prayer, we are building upon sand because we are depending on our own strength instead of that of God.

Contemplation

The key concept to understand the Carmelite way of following Jesus Christ is contemplation. It is very easy to neutralise that word by either making it too esoteric or too ordinary. Contemplation is not an experience of bliss given to some pure and chosen souls. Neither is it simply an attitude that we put on like we put on a jacket. It means to grow in intimacy with Jesus Christ, surrendering ourselves completely to him. Gradually he purifies and transforms us and we begin to see as God sees and love as God loves. On this journey we must be prepared to let lesser gods die so that we can receive the True God. We will not be able to let go of lesser loves unless we have known a deeper love. The false self does not want to die and will be continually whispering in our ears that that there is no need to take things so seriously, that we must have this or that for our happiness.

Contemplation begins when we entrust ourselves to God, whatever way God chooses to come to us.[4] However we need to stay awake and recognise the approach of God who may come to us in totally unexpected ways. Mary received the Word of God through the message of an angel but was also open to hearing God's voice at the foot of the cross. Elijah met God not in the earthquake or the fire or the mighty wind but in the sound of sheer silence. (I Kings 19,11-13)

If we accept God's invitation to begin the interior journey, we will of course meet with difficulties on the way because we will be brought face to face with ourselves. We will see ever more clearly the motives for our actions. We will see that sometimes even our best actions have selfish motives. This is very difficult to accept and this is why the spiritual journey is so difficult and why many might wish to turn back to a less challenging place. If, however we but knew the gift God was offering us, we would continue our journey despite the painful revelations about ourselves which we were offered. On this journey we become less proud, less sure of our own virtue but more reliant on the mercy of God and more aware that all human beings are our brothers and sisters.

Our world is undergoing great cultural upheaval. There is a profound spiritual crisis in our times. What have we to say in this situation? The call to be contemplative is a vocation that affects the world. Contemplatives can be found in every walk of life. To be a contemplative is to respond in faith to a call from God who often seems to be hidden. In the midst of conflict and division, such people are tabernacles of God's presence, through whom God is powerfully present. Therefore in the present situation of our world, we can use whatever skills we have been given for the good of others but, above all, we can respond to the still small voice that calls us into an intimate relationship with Jesus Christ, the only Son of the Father. This is not a cosy intimacy but through the relationship with God, we will be gradually transformed to become what God knows we can be and be totally available for the divine work in the world. Mary was totally available for God. She is our model, our Mother and our Sister, accompanying us and encouraging us to believe always in God's promises, especially when appearances seem most discouraging.

Mary realised that all authority and dominion belonged to God and that God had chosen her for a particular task. Her prayer in Luke's Gospel expresses her contemplative understanding of how God is acting in the world for its salvation.

> *And Mary said, "My soul magnifies the Lord,*
> *47 and my spirit rejoices in God my Savior,*
> *48 for he has looked with favor on the lowliness of his servant. Surely, from now on all generations will call me blessed;*
> *49 for the Mighty One has done great things for me, and holy is his name.*

50 His mercy is for those who fear him from generation to generation.

51 He has shown strength with his arm; he has scattered the proud in the thoughts of their hearts.

52 He has brought down the powerful from their thrones, and lifted up the lowly;

53 he has filled the hungry with good things, and sent the rich away empty.

54 He has helped his servant Israel, in remembrance of his mercy,

55 according to the promise he made to our ancestors, to Abraham and to his descendants forever.

Can we discover the presence of God everywhere even in the midst of our world, which at times can be full of evil? This is the faith of Our Lady in the Magnificat who praises God for throwing down the proud, feeding the hungry and sending the rich away empty when most people would see the opposite as true. A contemplative is able to see beyond the externals to the reality beneath. A constant attitude of openness to God is of course not easy because the presence of God calls into question how we live and constantly calls us to conversion, which means change and we are not always very keen to change.

In the infancy narratives, Luke is not just concerned with facts but with the meaning of the facts. He is writing history in the biblical manner, which means the story of the mighty actions of God. The infancy narrative in Luke's Gospel is dominated by the idea of the messiah as the fulfilment of God's promises to Israel. When she is told of Elizabeth's pregnancy, Mary goes in haste to the hill country to a town in Judah (1,39). If the ancient tradition of placing Elizabeth's home in Ain Karim is correct, this would have been a journey of about four days. When Elizabeth sees Mary, she is filled with the Holy Spirit, and cries out in recognition that Mary is *"the mother of my Lord"* (1,43). The people of God cried out when they welcomed the ark of the presence of God (1 Chr. 15,28; 2 Chr.5,13). David exclaimed, *"How can the ark of the Lord come to me?"* (2 Sam.6,9). Elizabeth's welcome seems to confirm Mary's experience and the Magnificat is an explosion of joy.

The Magnificat is full of Old Testament allusions and has a special connection to the canticle of Hannah (1 Sam 2,1-10), who rejoices in the birth of her son, Samuel:

> *and as she worshiped the LORD, she said: "My heart exults in the LORD, my horn is exalted in my God. I have swallowed up my enemies; I rejoice in my victory.*
>
> *2 There is no Holy One like the LORD; there in no Rock like our God.*
>
> *3 "Speak boastfully no longer, nor let arrogance issue from your mouths. For an all-knowing God is the LORD, a God who judges deeds.*
>
> *4 The bows of the mighty are broken, while the tottering gird on strength.*
>
> *5 The well-fed hire themselves out for bread, while the hungry batten on spoil. The barren wife bears seven sons, while the mother of many languishes.*
>
> *6 "The LORD puts to death and gives life; he casts down to the nether world; he raises up again.*

7 The LORD makes poor and makes rich, he humbles, he also exalts.

8 He raises the needy from the dust; from the ash heap he lifts up the poor, To seat them with nobles and make a glorious throne their heritage. He gives to the vower his vow, and blesses the sleep of the just. "For the pillars of the earth are the LORD'S, and he has set the world upon them.

9 He will guard the footsteps of his faithful ones, but the wicked shall perish in the darkness. For not by strength does man prevail;

10 the LORD'S foes shall be shattered. The Most High in heaven thunders; The LORD judges the ends of the earth, Now may he give strength to his king, and exalt the horn of his anointed!"

Whatever its origin, Luke's attribution of the Magnificat to Mary gives us his idea of the depths of her faith. Elizabeth had blessed Mary as the mother of the messiah because she believed that the promise made to her would be fulfilled (Lk.1,45) and Mary gives the glory to God in joyful thanksgiving.

The Magnificat is a song of thanksgiving that celebrates the history of salvation from three perspectives. The first part (1,48-50) is the dialogue between the holy and faithful God and the humility and openness of the believer, represented in Luke's Gospel by Mary. In the second part (1, 51-53) there is an historical confirmation of the saving action of God. What God will do in the future is guaranteed by what He has done in the past. From that sure base there arises a firm hope for a new world where the usual schemes of this world will be overturned. All of this is founded upon the faithfulness of God who does not lead astray. The third part (1, 54-55) tells of God's saving intervention in the forthcoming birth of the messiah. God has been faithful to the promises made to Israel.

Proclaiming the Word of God

Every Christian shares in the threefold role of Jesus Christ: priest, prophet and king. A prophet is one who proclaims the Word of God. Christ **is** the Word of God. We must allow the Word to become part of us and allow God to speak through us. We too must become a word from God to our world. Mary received the Word in her heart and in her womb: *Behold the servant of the Lord. Be it done to me according to your word.* (Lk. 1, 38). The prophets of the Old Testament were all people of great faith. It is sufficient to remember the example of our father Elijah, who proclaimed the drought (I Kings 17,1) and then foretold when it would end (I Kings 18, 44). He gathered all the people on Mount Carmel and challenged them to stop hobbling first on one foot and then on the other, either believe in Baal or Yahweh, and then follow whoever is God. (I Kings 18, 21). Our choices have consequences. In sight of the whole people, he prayed and his sacrifice was accepted by the Lord (I Kings 18, 36-38).

Mary is the woman of faith and represents the faithful believer for Luke. Elisabeth recognises her faith and declares it to be the cause of her blessedness. Mary believed that what was said to her by the Lord would be fulfilled. In the first few lines of the Magnificat, Mary gives glory to God and rejoices in God her saviour. She declares that God has looked upon her lowliness. Therefore all generations will call her blessed. In the eyes of the important and powerful people, Mary would not have counted since she is a poor woman, but God's way of looking is very different from the way human beings look. We tend to see the exterior and base judgements on that. God sees the interior, the heart, and responds to that. Mary is aware that God is all-powerful and has done great things in her. She then goes on to recount the works of God throughout history.

God shows mercy to those who fear Him. Fear of the Lord is a normal biblical expression that does not refer to the emotion of fear but is a way of describing a right relationship of the human being with God, who is the Holy One. God is distinct from everything else that can exist and is the Creator of all. The person who recognises the sovereignty of God and tries to keep His commandments is the one who fears God. Such a person can depend on receiving mercy from God who is constant throughout the ages. One thing that fascinates me about the rest of the Magnificat is that the verb is in the past tense. Mary rejoices in what God has done: shown might with His arm, dispersed the proud and arrogant, thrown down the rulers and lifted up the lowly, filled the hungry with good things and sent the rich away empty. Is all that really true? Has God done all those things? Isn't it a fact that the proud and arrogant continue along their path believing in nothing outside of themselves? Is it not

Mary Obedient to the Word

a fact that the rulers continue to rule from their lofty thrones and the lowly are continually downtrodden? Is it not a fact that the hungry remain hungry and the rich get even richer?

A prophet receives a word from God for the world. The prophet must be open to receive the word and fearless in proclaiming it. A true prophet proclaims God's word and not his or her own. Those who work in the area of justice and peace tend to have an awareness of some of the great injustices of our day and want to do something about these situations. This is very laudable but we must seek to be aware of who we are trying to help. Is it the poor and downtrodden or is it ourselves? In St. John's Gospel, there is a famous scene where Mary of Bethany pours out very costly ointment over the head of Jesus. Judas protests about this colossal waste of money that could have been used to benefit the poor.

> *Jn. 12, 5 "Why was this oil not sold for three hundred days' wages and given to the poor?"*
> *6 He said this not because he cared about the poor but because he was a thief and held the moneybag and used to steal the contributions.*

Not all comments in favour of the poor are prophetic. We have to be careful that our work and statements on behalf of the poor are in fact for the poor.

The false self is ever ready to spoil our good intentions and to twist them to its own purposes. The false self seeks its own security, survival and esteem and will seek these wherever they are to be found. Therefore we must have a constant guard of our heart that what we say and what we do are according to the will of God and not according to what will make us look good and feel good. In the Carmelite Rule, we are warned to

> *use every care to clothe yourselves in God's armour so that you may be ready to withstand the enemy's ambush (Rule, 18).*

One of the parts of this divine armour is faith:

> *Faith must be your shield on all occasions, and with it you will be able to quench the flaming missiles of the wicked one (Eph. 6, 16): there can be no pleasing God without faith (Heb. 11, 6); and the victory lies in this – your faith (cf. I Jn. 5,4).*

Faith is not just holding the correct set of beliefs; it is a personal relationship with God in Jesus Christ, in which we "fear the Lord", in the sense of realising that God is God and that by grace alone can we enter such a relationship. Faith means to accept God as God chooses to reveal Himself to us. God has loved the world so much as to enter it in a new way in His Son, Jesus Christ. God has stooped down to us in order to lift us up. God has taken on our human weakness in order to transform it. Every human being reveals something of God to those with eyes to see and ears and hearts that are open. In Jesus we encounter the help of God under the form of poverty. God takes on our poverty and shares his own riches with us. (2 Cor.8, 9). In order to participate in the riches of Christ, it is necessary also to participate in the mystery of poverty and of self-emptying, which is fully revealed to us in the death of Jesus on the cross. God reveals his power in powerlessness (2 Cor. 12,9-10; 1 Cor. 1,25).

Mary was open to the transforming action of God because she recognised her own nothingness. St. Paul understood that it was when he was weak that he was strong. (2 Cor. 12, 10). However in the first letter to the Corinthians, (1, 27), he declares,

> *Rather, God chose the foolish of the world to shame the wise,*
> *and God chose the weak of the world to shame the strong,*
> *28 and God chose the lowly and despised of the world, those*
> *who count for nothing, to reduce to nothing those who are something,*
> *29 so that no human being might boast before God.*

St. Thérèse of Lisieux knew that her nothingness attracted God's gaze and therefore she believed that her seemingly fantastic hopes would be fulfilled, not because of anything she could do but because of God's loving mercy. Mary believed in the power of God and that God's power has already accomplished what He has promised from of old. All pride will be thrown down. Those who have trusted in God will find that their trust has not been misplaced. Those who hunger and thirst for God will be filled. However, she proclaims that this victory has already taken place because of the imminent coming of the messiah, her son, Jesus. All those promises made to Abraham and his children, have now been fulfilled in Christ.

In the rest of the Gospel of Luke, Jesus proclaims a new world order, not based on violent revolution but on a change of heart. In his inaugural sermon in the synagogue in Nazareth, he sets out his programme from the Prophet Isaiah

> *The Spirit of the Lord is upon me, because he has anointed me to bring glad tidings to the poor. He has sent me to proclaim liberty to captives and recovery of sight to the blind, to let the oppressed go free,*
> 19 *and to proclaim a year acceptable to the Lord. (4, 18-19).*

Mary's prophecy in the Magnificat is beginning to come true. Wherever Jesus goes he expels demons and sickness. He even forgives sins (Lk. 5, 20). All these things represent the bonds that have imprisoned men and women. They are now broken but people must accept the new life that is offered to them. Humanity does all in its power to kill this new life but Jesus is raised from the dead to eternal life that is offered to all people.

Sharing in the eternal life of God means to live the life of God. It means to see as God sees and to love as God loves. God has already thrown down the arrogant, deposed the rulers and raised up the lowly. We, the followers of Jesus Christ, must carry out his vision and his programme of action. We must bring the Good News of the Kingdom to the poor. We can only do that with the faith and obedience that Mary exemplifies. That faith must drive us and motivate all our actions so that we do not simply hear the Word of God but like Mary also put it into practice (Lk. 8, 21).

Endnotes

1. See KLEMENS STOCK, *Mary the Mother of the Lord in the New Testament*, (Edizioni Carmelitane, Rome, 2006) and JOSEPH CHALMERS, *Let It Be* (St. Albert's Press, Faversham, expected in 2010)
2. *Gaudium et Spes* 1
3. *Way of Perfection* 21,2
4. Cf. *Constitutions of the Carmelite Friars*, 17.

THE FUTURE OF OUR PAST
THE SCAPULAR
FOR THE THIRD MILLENNIUM

The scapular devotion has a long history and others are more qualified than I am to delve into the past. For our present purposes I am more interested in the present and the future as the title of this chapter might indicate. Whatever is the history that lies behind the scapular devotion, the fact is that it is an important symbol in Carmelite spirituality. We simply cannot understand Carmelite devotion to Our Lady without reference to the scapular. Indeed for centuries the scapular summed up the whole of Carmelite Marian devotion.

The present reality regarding the scapular devotion varies widely according to culture and temperament. For many years the scapular was handed out to all and sundry with very little and even no explanation. In his letter to mark the Carmelite Marian year, Pope John Paul II made it very clear that first and foremost the scapular is a "habit", that is the official religious garment worn by the Carmelite friars.[1] The scapular that most people wear is a miniature version of the Carmelite habit. The Pope wrote that wearing the scapular brings one into relationship with the Carmelite Order in some way and therefore into contact with the whole body of Carmelite spirituality. Regarding the future of the scapular devotion, one of the challenges facing the Carmelite Order is to offer an effective explanation of its meaning in the modern age.

We know that for all sorts of reasons, devotion to Our Lady underwent a crisis after the Second Vatican Council. At the same time, symbols of all kinds also entered into a crisis. A symbol is something which points to and represents a profound reality. A road sign points the right way on the road but it is not a symbol since it does not represent in itself the right way. The scapular points to Our Lady and in fact represents a profound relationship to her as Mother, Sister and Patroness. The scapular devotion suffered attacks from three separate fronts: the first was the historical problems surrounding the beginnings of the devotion. The famous scapular vision, from an historical point of view, can neither be proved nor disproved; the so-called sabbatine privilege has been shown not to have any historical basis. The second front was the general crisis of symbols where what had been meaningful for a previous generation suddenly was not so clear to another generation. The third front was the crisis in Marian devotion in general. This last crisis has lessened somewhat and now most Catholics would admit to having some sort of relationship with Our Lady. The kind of relationship often depends on culture or taste.

I do not believe that there is one single meaning for the scapular in the third millennium. The scapular is the symbol of a relationship with Mary, who is our Mother, our Sister and our Patroness. These three elements involve very different kinds of relationships. One relates very differently to a mother and a sister. Everyone has a different relationship to his or her mother. Some people have a very tender relationship with their mother while others have troubled relationships despite the love which binds them together. The way of expressing Marian devotion differs greatly from culture to culture and one must be very wary of judging devotion only from an external point of view. A very deep devotion may or may not have an exuberant exterior.

The spiritual meaning of the scapular

I am not so much interested in how the scapular devotion is expressed from an external point of view; that depends on so many personal factors. What does concern me is the spiritual meaning of wearing the scapular in the third millennium. The Pope, in his letter to the Order, placed Carmelite Marian devotion within the context of the devotion of the whole Church to Mary and the place that she has been given by God in the mystery of Christ and the Church. He said that the scapular devotion is a treasure for the whole Church and that it has two fundamental elements: on the one hand, the scapular is a reminder of Our Lady's constant care and protection throughout the whole of our lives and at the moment of our passage from this world into eternity; on the other hand, it is a reminder also of the necessity of imitating Mary. When we put on the scapular, we remind ourselves about the need to take on her virtues.

The idea that the scapular in some way guarantees entry into heaven comes from a medieval idea that perseverance in the religious life is a sign that the person will go to heaven. I have already mentioned that Pope John Paul II stressed that the scapular is essentially the habit, which Carmelite friars and nuns wear, although in miniature form; so wearing it faithfully is comparable to persevering in the religious life. In the Middle Ages, there was great concern and fear over one's eternal salvation. We tend to have different ideas today. Because of our knowledge of psychology, which was not available to medieval people, we are now aware that one can remain or leave religious life for all sorts of reasons. It is not always a good thing that someone stay in religious life and it is not always a bad thing that someone leaves. Only God can judge; we cannot read the human heart. We also tend to have some different ideas of God and most people do not believe that God is just waiting for us to infringe one of the many rules so that we can be plunged for all eternity into hell fire where we will writhe in the searing flames that will have no end. There now tends to be more stress on the infinite mercy of God.

St. Thérèse of Lisieux had some wonderful insights into the nature of God. She believed that God was her Father who loved her without measure. She believed that God was merciful because he was just. Her understanding was that

God can read our hearts, knows what our motives were for all our actions and so as a just judge takes everything into account. Of course it is possible that our modern understanding of God veers too far to the merciful side. However, I invite you to read once again the parable, popularly known as the Prodigal Son in St. Luke's Gospel and tell me then that God is not merciful. One day St. Therese was having a discussion with another nun about God. The other nun was frightened of God and feared God's judgement. Therese tried to talk to her about the mercy of God but nothing would move the nun. Finally Therese became exasperated with her and said, "Sister, if you want justice, you will get justice. If you want mercy, you will get mercy."

It is important to understand that the scapular is not a magic passport into heaven. We may have the passport but we still need the right visa! The visa is that we have sought to live according to God's will insofar as we have understood it. Jesus said, *"Those to whom much has been give, much more will be required"*. There are some people, who because of their upbringing, have very little knowledge of God and there are others, who have been given every benefit of a good religious background. What will be expected of each person differs.

The scapular is also not a magic talisman that protects us from all harm. Our Lady does protect us but does not take us out of the world. At the last supper, Jesus prayed for his followers, saying to the Father, *"I do not ask you to take them out of the world, but to guard them from the evil one."* (Jn. 17, 15). Some of the hard knocks of life are actually for our benefit; we often are not aware of that at the time but only later.

So if wearing the scapular does not guarantee us a place in heavenly glory, nor is it a foolproof insurance policy against getting knocked down on the road, why should we bother wearing it? What has it possibly got to say to people of the third millennium?

The scapular is a reminder of Mary's commitment to us and our commitment to Mary. It is a reminder of her constant presence in our lives and her interest in us. She really is a Mother and a Sister, leading us and guiding us to Christ her Son in whom we find salvation. There are many sons and daughters of earthly mothers who make a big splash on Mother's Day with flowers and chocolates but who cannot be bothered with their mothers throughout the rest of the year. Chocolates and flowers are very nice but if there is no regular contact to back them up, their significance gets watered down. Some people express their devotion to Our Lady with outward signs and that is fine so long as these signs emerge from a real relationship with her. Jesus heavily criticised the Pharisees because of their outward displays of religion that had no basis in reality. If the outward signs are just a passing emotion, they will have no lasting impact on our lives.

If we are true children of Mary, we will be willing to learn from her. In St. John's Gospel, Our Lady plays a pivotal role. She does not appear very often but her appearances are at crucial times. She is present at the beginning of Jesus' public ministry at the marriage feast of Cana, and at the end of his public ministry at the foot of the cross, when she becomes the Mother of all believers. She is responsible for hastening the beginning of the public ministry, when she points out to her Son that they have run out of wine. Jesus tells her that it has nothing to do with them but she knows her Son very well; she is not put off by his words. In fact she goes to the servants and tells them to do whatever he tells them. We know that Jesus told them to fill the huge wine jars with water, which would have been a very laborious task. Some biblical expert has worked out that about 120 gallons of water were turned into wine that day! The servants did what Jesus told them to do, even though it must have seemed futile, and their obedience and faith in him were repaid a hundredfold.

Our Lady always points us to Jesus and continually reminds us to do whatever he tells us. Sometimes we may be tempted to think that what the Lord wants of us does not make much sense, like loving our neighbour and forgiving not seven times but seventy times seven and so on. However, if we seek to put the message of Jesus into practice day in and day out, we will discover that we will be repaid a hundredfold. God is never outdone in generosity.

From the cross, Jesus gave the beloved disciple to Our Lady to be her son. The beloved disciple is a representative figure, representing all Christians. All of us have been given into the care of Mary, our Mother. Equally, Jesus told the beloved disciple, representing us, to take Mary as his own mother. John's Gospel tells us that he took her into his own home. This is an invitation also to us, to take Mary into our hearts and to establish with her an intimate relationship of Mother and son or daughter.

Mary's appearances in the other Gospels are infrequent but very important. We learn a great deal about her from them. When we put on the scapular, we are committing ourselves also to put on her virtues. We learn from the Gospels that she is a woman of faith, a disciple of her Son; she is humble, which means simply to know and accept the truth about oneself; she is silent, "pondering all these things in her heart".

The mysteries of Mary

From very early on in the history of the Order, Our Lady was understood as the model of all that the Carmelite hoped and aspired to be. A favourite title for Our Lady within Carmel was "Most Pure Virgin" and this was understood as referring to the fact that she belonged totally to God. No sin existed in her. We are sinners of course but the sinless state of Mary is a vision of our future. It is also a spur to do all in our power to lead lives that are according to the Gospel.

Another mystery that attracted Carmelites was Mary carrying the divine child in her womb. The thrust of Carmelite life is to be united with God and no clearer union with God could be imagined than that which Mary had with God's only Son. Despite the fact that Our Lady is unlike us in that she was completely sinless and had a unique relationship with God, nevertheless Carmelites saw in her the fullest expression of what they aspired to be. They never saw her as distant or untouchable because of her privileges; instead, because of their traditional understanding of Our Lady as their Patroness, Mother and Sister, Carmelites always tended to have a close and intimate relationship with her. All of this relationship is summed up and represented in the symbol of the scapular.

Blessed Titus Brandsma, the Carmelite who was martyred in Dachau concentration camp in 1942, had profound insights into the Carmelite's relationship with Our Blessed Lady. He understood that the Carmelite was called to be another Mary. By this he meant that what happened in Our Lady's life was a pattern for our lives. Think of the Annunciation scene in St. Luke's Gospel. (Lk. 1, 26-38). Of course what happened to Our Lady was unique but nevertheless we can also learn something about ourselves from this mystery. Mary was asked to become the mother of the long promised messiah and when she asked how this could come about because she was a virgin, she was told that God's power would accomplish this great work. What was required of her, something that God could not produce, was her consent. She consented to the presence and action of God in her life and because of her "yes" the Word became flesh and dwelt amongst us.

The Christian vocation and something that Carmelite spirituality particularly focuses on, is to be transformed in God. Our limited human ways of thinking, loving and acting will be transformed into divine ways, that is our way of relating to the whole of creation must be changed radically so that each of us becomes another expression of God through our own humanity. At present our sin disfigures the presence of God in our lives. Titus' idea is that, like Mary we too must welcome the Word of God into our lives and pronounce our "yes". This "yes" has profound effects in our lives. Imagine if you opened the door to a friend and invited that person in to your home to live with you. It might be lovely for a little while to have your friend around but gradually the novelty would wear off and little things would begin to jangle your nerves. Accepting the Word of God in your life in a sense is like getting married. How long does it take for the honeymoon phase to pass? So we need to repeat our "yes" many times over. Mary said yes in the joy of the annunciation but repeated it at the foot of the cross as she watched her only Son die seemingly a failure.

The Word of God grew within Mary. Being a mere man, I would not presume to suggest that I understood what goes on in the heart of a pregnant woman but I believe that it is not all joy and bliss. I think that the growing child within the womb can also cause various discomforts for the woman. Welcoming the Word into our lives will also demand things of us that can be uncomfortable. We will no longer be able to continue our feud with our neighbour; our unchristian attitudes and ideas will be challenged. If the Word of God is going to grow in our lives, we must repeat our consent to the presence and action of God even when this proves to be uncomfortable to us. If we are serious about the business of letting God into our lives, we will begin to experience God's presence in various ways throughout the day. By experiencing God's presence, I do not mean that we will have lovely feelings of bliss. Instead we will begin to be aware of what needs to be transformed in our lives since the presence of God will show up what is false. We will begin to become aware that we are a brother or a sister of everyone, even and perhaps especially of those to whom we are not attracted at all. God is love and where God is, love grows.

Welcoming the Word of God into our lives is a gradual process. It does not happen overnight and we need to be patient with ourselves as well as with others. At the same time, we must not presume too easily that God's will has been totally accomplished in and through us. We are on the way. Mary, our Patroness, our Mother and our Sister, accompanies us on this long journey, which reaches its destination in eternity.

The scapular then is not a good luck charm or a guarantee of heaven no matter the kind of life one has lived. It is a symbol, representing a profound relationship between the wearer and Our Lady. It is the Carmelite habit in miniature and therefore the one who wears the scapular, becomes a Carmelite in some way. The wearer of the scapular should be encouraged to get to know the immensely rich and varied relationship between Carmel and Mary. The scapular is a reminder of the continual presence of Our Lady "who watches over with loving care the brothers and sisters of her Son" (*Preface of the Solemn Commemoration of Our Lady of Mount Carmel*). She is the Patroness of Carmelites, and as such has always been understood to protect the Order. She is Mother and cares for us with a mother's love, nurturing the divine life within us and helping us to become what God created us to be. She is our Sister, who accompanies us always and is always there for us. The scapular is then a reminder of Our Lady's commitment to us but it is also a reminder of our commitment to her. When we put on the scapular, we take upon ourselves the sweet and gentle yoke of Christ. We commit ourselves to put the Gospel into practice in our daily lives and learn from the example of Our Lady who is the first and perfect disciple of her Son.

The scapular is a very simple devotion, perhaps too simple for the taste of some people. It is the symbol of a Mother's care for her children and of the child's love for its Mother. In the third millennium, as in other ages, how we express our relationship with Our Lady will differ according to culture. The scapular, which has been a powerful symbol in the past, can speak just as powerfully to people of this time and be a constant reminder of the place of Our Lady within the Christian life and within the life of each individual. She is our Patroness, our Mother and our Sister. She points us towards Christ and accompanies us on our journey. She desires our salvation more than we do ourselves and so she constantly reminds us to *"do whatever he tells you"*. (Jn. 2,5)

Endnotes

1   The full text of this letter can be found in Joseph Chalmers, *Mary the Contemplative,* (Edizioni Carmelitane, Rome, 2001, Appendix One).

THE LORD HEARS THE CRY OF THE POOR

Poverty, the desert and the Carmelite charism

The formation document of the Carmelite Order, the RIVC says,

> "The authentic contemplative journey allows us to discover our own frailty, our weakness, our poverty - in a word, the nothingness of human nature: all is grace. Through this experience, we grow in solidarity with those who live in situations of deprivation and injustice. As we allow ourselves to be challenged by the poor and by the oppressed, we are gradually transformed, and we begin to see the world with God's eyes and to love the world with his heart. (cf. Constitutions of the friars, 15). With God, we hear the cry of the poor, (Ex. 3,7) and we strive to share the Divine solicitude, concern, and compassion for the poorest and the least." (No. 43)

The United Nations declared 2006 to be the year of the desert in order to get the message across that their continuing loss is a major problem for humanity and to protect the unique eco-system and cultural diversity of deserts worldwide.[1] The desert is of course an important biblical symbol and plays a vital part in the Carmelite spiritual tradition. It speaks to us of the journey towards God and reminds us particularly of Elijah's journey towards Mount Horeb (I Kings 19, 4-8), when Elijah took the same road as did Moses in order to encounter God.

In the Bible, both poverty and the desert express a harsh reality of people's lives. At the same time, they are also symbols for the long journey that the people must accomplish in obedience to the mission they have received from God. The desert is the place of utter poverty, crisis, of fleeing, complaining, struggling and temptation, where the people discovered their own interior poverty, their limits, and their weaknesses. The poverty of the desert is also the place from where the people escape to freedom. They journeyed for forty years towards the sources of their faith, where they rediscovered their memory and their identity. The desert is where the remains of Pharaoh's oppression are left behind and where the people learn to live fraternally. It is the place where they meet their God once again, the place of the covenant, of a renewed commitment, of prayer, of rediscovering the presence of God as a completely free gift. (cf. Hos. 2, 16-17; Ex. 5, 1.3)

The experience of the desert marked the life of the Prophet Elijah. He confronted the deserts of Karith (1Kings 17,5), of Beersheba (1Kings 19, 4), of Horeb (1Kings 19,8). The desert is not only a geographic place, but also is an interior experience. In the desert Elijah experienced his own poverty (1Kings 19, 4-5). He did not reach the point of losing his faith but he did not know how to utilise the faith he had inherited to confront a new situation. The interior desert, his crisis, showed itself in the fact that he sought the presence of God in the traditional signs (earthquake, mighty wind, great fire) and he discovered that these signs no longer revealed anything about God. (1Kings 19,11-12). The experience of the desert on Mount Carmel deeply marked the life of the first Carmelites. Leaving Palestine, they carried with them, within themselves, the Carmelite desert. Living in Europe, they met the desert once again, not in the regular life of the large independent monasteries, far from the cities, but in the poor style of life of mendicant communities, close to the poor and in the cities. Poverty and the desert taken together can express the profound meaning of the Carmelite charism.

The RIVC has this to say about the journey through the desert:

> *The first Carmelites, in tune with the spirituality of their time (the 12th-13th centuries), attempted to live out this ascetic commitment by withdrawing into solitude. Their desert was more than a physical reality; it was a place of the heart…..In the footsteps of the first Carmelite hermits, we too journey through the desert, which develops our contemplative dimension. This requires self-abandonment to a gradual process of emptying and stripping ourselves, so that we may be clothed in Christ and filled with God. This process "begins when we entrust ourselves to God, in whatever way he chooses to approach us" (Constitutions of the friars, no. 17). For we do not enter the desert by our own will: it is the Holy Spirit who calls us and draws us into the desert; it is the Spirit who sustains us in our spiritual combat, clothes us in God's armour (cf. Rule, 18-19) and*

> *fills us with his gifts and with the divine presence, until we are entirely transformed by God and reflect something of God's infinite beauty. (see St. John of the Cross, Canticle B, 36,5 and 2Cor. 3, 18). (No. 27)*

Poverty in the Old Testament

In the Old Testament, poverty is an evil against which one must struggle and ask God to be set free (Dt. 15, 7-11). The consequences of poverty are humiliation, oppression, and dependence (Sir. 13, 3-7. 21-23). From this comes the evil. God, who made a covenant with the Chosen People, has a particular care for the disinherited, widows, slaves and orphans (Ex. 22, 25-26; Lv. 25, 35-38; Dt. 24, 10-15). Some people were so burdened by debt that they saw no option but to sell themselves into slavery. The law of the covenant protected them and defended them against cruelty so that if a slave was injured in the eye or lost a tooth, the master was obliged to set the slave free. (Ex.21, 1-11.21.26-27; Dt. 15, 12-15)). The Israelites experienced in Egypt the weight of servitude. They were foreigners serving the local people. God intervened and brought the people out of Egypt. This was a profound experience for them that remained foundational. (Ex.21,20). However, it took forty years of wandering in the desert before they were ready to enter the Promised Land. When they began to settle down, they had to learn that the foreigner is poor and that God loves him too. The widow and orphan are in the same situation, as they have no protection against injustice and mistreatment (Ex.22, 21-23). It was believed that God hears the cry of the poor, those who suffer and the humiliated (Ex. 2, 24; 3,7; Sir. 4,1-6; 21,5). The messiah king will protect the poor. (Is. 11, 4; Ps. 34,7). God takes the side of the poor, of the victims of injustice, the persecuted, and the weak:

For he has not spurned nor disdained
the wretched man in his misery.
Nor did he turn his face away from him. (Ps. 22,25).

Initially, above all starting from the period of the monarchy, the appearance of poor people was a challenge to the existing mindset. The simple fact of there being poor people was believed to be an indication that the covenant had been broken. The prophets became spokesmen for the demands of divine justice. Among them, the Prophet Elijah holds a special place I Kings 21,17-22; 2Chr. 21,11-15). Later, especially during the Babylonian captivity, when the whole people were oppressed and poor, those who found themselves in such a position were no longer to be assisted simply by receiving alms from those who were rich, but it was understood that the poor themselves had a mission to accomplish with regard to the Chosen People and with regard even to the whole of humanity. This mission is expressed clearly in the songs of the Servant of Yahweh (Is. 42,6-7; 49,6; 61,1), which shaped Jesus' understanding of his mission. (cf. Lk.4, 18 - 19).

Slowly, over the centuries, the term "poor" came not only to express a social or political status but also it is understood to be an interior attitude of faithfulness that often brings with it isolation and persecution by the powerful. The little book of Zephaniah affirms that the opposite of poverty is not wealth but pride. The poor are humbly submissive to the will of God. (Zeph.2,3) Yahweh's poor (the anawim) are the object of his benevolent love (cf. Is. 49, 13; 66,2) and are the first fruits of the "humble and modest people" (Zeph. 3, 12) that the Messiah will gather together. God gives salvation to those who accept his will. Jeremiah was not an indigent prophet (Jer.32, 6-15) but he experienced persecution. From his experience of being despised, persecuted and being weak, Jeremiah learned trust in God and so he discovered the source of his salvation (Jer. 20,7-13). Jeremiah also is one of the poor of the Lord. Material poverty is not a value in itself but it does have a particular religious significance. It is a call to open oneself to God. It is a mysterious preparation to accept God as the giver of all things. As a spiritual attitude, the person is poor who, in a situation of need, seeks humbly the help of the Lord (cf. Ps. 34,7-11).

The idea that we find in the Law and the Prophets can also be found in the Wisdom Literature. The book of Job, for example, describes in a very lively way, the situation of the poor. (Job 24, 1-12) The psalms have a wonderful spirituality of the poor. There is a loving dialogue between the poor and God. The one who prays presents his own misery and suffering, abandoning himself to God (Jer. 20, 7-13). The poor look for their salvation to Yahweh on whom they depend. The danger of wealth is seen in the fact that it is the source of pride. (Ps.49, 17-18) For this reason there tends to be identification in the Bible between "rich" and "wicked". (Is.53,9). The rich person tends to be self-satisfied and proud and therefore does not believe in God. (Ps.52,9).The Lord will give justice to the humble and the poor. The justice of God is not that of strict law but comes from the promises of the covenant:

> *He raises up the lowly from the dust;*
> *from the dunghill he lifts up the poor*
> *To seat them with princes*
> *With the princes of his own people. (Ps. 113, 7)*

Poverty in the New Testament

The Gospel of St. Luke presents us with the figure of Mary as the epitome of the "anawim" (the poor ones of Yahweh). She trusted in God and believed that the promises made to her would be fulfilled (Lk. 1, 45). Mary is the "servant of the Lord" (Lk. 1,38), the only woman in the whole Bible so named. At the beginning of the New Testament, Mary brings the trust and faith of the anawim of the Old Testament to a new peak and she is declared to be "full of grace" (Lk. 1, 30) and "blessed among women" (Lk. 1. 42). The Magnificat (Lk. 1, 46-55) is a prophetic song of thanksgiving to God for the wonders that He has accomplished. It contains the core of the Gospel in a few words. Mary can see through the externals that surround her to the reality beneath. She proclaims the Good News of the Kingdom of God as already realised and so she sees that God's mercy extends from generation to generation to those who fear Him. She rejoices that God has shown his strength scattering the proud in the conceit of their hearts, putting down the mighty from their thrones and exalting the lowly. She proclaims that God has already filled the hungry with good things and sent the rich away empty. The Magnificat reveals that God is on the side of the lowly and the poor. When the Reign of God is fully established, these people will come into their inheritance. Those who trust in God's promises now will be amply rewarded.

In the Old Testament we do not meet a spirituality of renunciation. This comes with the lifestyle and spirit of Jesus. Material poverty is a sorrowful experience, but many poor people have accepted their condition with a complete trust in God. The example of Mary, who understood herself to be "the servant of the Lord" marked the life of her Son. He too defined himself in terms of service: *"The Son of Man has not come to be served but to serve and to give his life as a ransom for many."* (Mk. 10,45) In the synagogue at Nazareth, when he outlined his mission to the people, Jesus used a phrase from the Prophet Isaiah, taken from one of the summaries of the Songs of the Servant of Yahweh, where the prophet described the mission of the Messiah as the servant of the poor: *"The Spirit of the Lord is upon me and has anointed me to announce the good news to the poor, to proclaim liberty to captives, to restore sight to the blind, to set free those who are oppressed, and to proclaim the Lord's year of favour"*. (Lk. 4, 18-19)

The public ministry of Jesus was marked by itinerant preaching. The simple people followed him. They were fascinated by the power of his teaching (Mk. 1, 22. 27). He chose a group of disciples who followed him, in his way of life as well as in his teaching (cf. Lk. 10, 1-9). The Jewish teachers taught the Law and its interpretation. They did so in a fixed place, were surrounded by students, men only. Jesus was also called "master" (rabbi). However, Jesus did not belong to any of the schools of the Jewish teachers. The doctrine of Jesus did not come from any particular school or course of study. What he taught came from his own experience of intimate dialogue with the Father (Jn. 5,19. 30; 15,15). There was amazement at his learning (Jn.7,15. 46). Jesus overcame the abyss between the learned doctors of the Law and the simple people (Mt. 11, 28).

Jesus lived in uncertainty, in a precarious situation. He lived without a home, as a stranger and pilgrim on the earth. Following him means facing an existence deprived of human security and characterised by poverty (Mt. 8,20). The disciples of the Master do not have permission to establish themselves comfortably in this world. (Lk. 9,57-58). The disciples are called to take risks and to live a precarious existence, uncertain, insecure on a material level and even more so on a spiritual level, in the sense that they have to let go of their lives in order to receive life in abundance. (Mt. 16, 25). The radical poverty of Jesus consists in his self-emptying. (Phil.2,7). In Jesus we meet the help of God under the form of poverty. God takes on our poverty and shares his own riches with us. (2Cor.8,9). Of course the riches of God have nothing to do with money. In order to participate in the riches of Christ, it is necessary also to participate in the mystery of poverty and of self-emptying, which is fully revealed to us in the death of Jesus on the cross. God reveals his power in powerlessness (2Cor. 12,9-10; 1Cor. 1,25).

Jesus fully accepted our human condition (Heb. 2,17; Rom. 8,3). He took upon himself our weakness. (Mt.8,17). He lived a life of obedience even to death on a cross. Jesus did not impose himself with violence. On the contrary, he is with the humble and poor. His yoke is easy and his burden light. (Mt. 11, 30) We are called to imitate him in his attitude of compassionate and merciful love towards the humble and the lost. (Mt.11,28). Those who are poor like Jesus, pour out love without counting the cost. The generosity of the poor widow is contrasted with the avarice of the scribes and the proud rich people. (Mk.12,41-44). On the other hand, even the disciples protested at the woman who poured out the costly ointment on Jesus. (Mt. 26,8-9). Whoever is seduced and attracted by the love of Christ, gives away everything, sharing his poverty and experiencing his generosity (Mk. 10,28).

Wealth is not condemned but its value is relativised and human beings are warned to use it wisely and moderately. The Sermon on the Mount is fundamental to the concept of Christian poverty (Mt. 5, 3-12; Lk. 6,20-38). In this famous sermon, Jesus lays out the fundamental values of God's Reign. Luke's Gospel has *"blessed you who are poor"* (6,20) as the first beatitude while Matthew has *"blessed are the poor in spirit"*. (5, 3). The poor, because of their situation, have no one else but God on whom to depend. The poor are meek and humble of heart. They are the most likely to hear the message of Jesus. There is a spiritual character to poverty as availability for the Gospel, and as an interior renunciation of trying to save oneself and relying on God. Poverty in spirit includes an interior emptiness, a waiting that can only be assuaged by God in Jesus Christ. Those who are aware of their human lack, awaiting all things from God, are poor in spirit (cf. Lk. 12,33-34).

Christ invites us to abandon ourselves into the hands of the Father, trusting to live today, as a gift of God's goodness and love. We are not alone but walk in the presence of the providential love of the Father. Freedom from anxiety and the preoccupations of daily life finds its justification in the fact that life is more than the material things that sustain it. God cares also for the flowers of the field. (Mt. 6, 28-30) It is stupid to be worried about life because human beings do not have power over it. Trusting in God is to seek the Kingdom. When our centre of gravity and our point of reference are the search for the Kingdom, which absorbs our energy and interest, we are set free from the preoccupations of life. The Kingdom is a gift of the Father to the little group of disciples and so they need not be afraid. (Lk.12,32). The Kingdom begins to take shape when the disciples put their goods at the disposition of the poor. The only way to rescue the human being from the bonds of material goods is to share them. (Lk.12,33).

To serve God and Mammon is not possible. (Lk.16,13). Mammon gives power over others and lays claim to goods that all have need of. It is not the same as simply money but refers to economic power that takes over the human heart. Mammon is an idol. It is always evil because it is the fruit of cupidity and is the source of false trust. The paradox of Christianity brings about a profound change of values. Christ is very severe regarding mammon because it can imprison the human heart and obscure the clear will of God toward one's neighbour. Adoration of mammon happens when people allow themselves to be seduced by material things. They multiply their possessions and their riches, desiring and exercising dominion over other people. On the other hand, giving away money and sharing it with the poor, they become friends and intercessors before God. Wealth has a demonic power since it tends to bind the human heart and makes it deaf to the call of God's Kingdom. St. Luke, in his parable of the rich man and Lazarus (Lk. 16, 19-31), stresses the vastly different destinies of the two men. The rich man, who is indifferent to the poor, ends up as a total and irreversible failure. The destiny of the poor man ends in communion of life with all the just. The Gospel does not condemn one economic condition or another. Jesus does warn about the lure of riches that can suffocate the seed of the Word and prevent it from bearing fruit. (Mk.4,19). For the one who is invited by Jesus to follow him, the Kingdom must be the absolute priority. In order to follow him, one must be prepared to sacrifice every other connection, even those of a family nature, and also all one's own plans and interests, if these interfere with the primary cause of the Reign of God (Mk. 8,34-35; 10,29-30).

Jesus and his disciples used material goods (Lk.8,3). What Jesus denounces as dangerous is the aspiration and the anxiety to accumulate wealth as a guarantee of life and of security. The source of life cannot be found in material things. The security of human life cannot be found in possessions. (Lk.12,15). The one way to be set free is to give away one's possessions (Mk. 10,21). The abandonment and the privation of goods, as an experience of liberty, are an invitation that Jesus makes to those who are willing to follow him. (Lk.12,22). Those who worry about material things, to the point of tormenting themselves, show that they have not yet discovered that the One who has given all - life - will also give the lesser things - food and clothing. Cupidity is an illness; it is an unsatisfied desire that anxiously seeks new and more numerous possessions, transforming life into a useless, insatiable and endless chain of unfulfilled desires (Ecc 5, 9-11).

Poverty in the Consecrated Life

All Carmelites look back to the founding experience of the small group of nameless hermits on Mount Carmel. They were laymen who simply wished to live in allegiance to Jesus Christ following an eremitical and penitential lifestyle in his own land. Somewhere between 1206 and 1214 they had achieved sufficient cohesion as a group to seek formal recognition by the Church and to receive some direction. St. Albert of Jerusalem gave them this by means of his letter, the "formula vitae". When the hermits received formal approval of the "formula vitae" by Pope Innocent IV in 1247, they became religious through the commonly accepted three vows. At present the Carmelite Family includes friars, cloistered nuns, hermits, sisters of apostolic life, all of whom make profession of the three vows of chastity, poverty and obedience, as well as many lay Carmelites, some of whom also take vows although most do not.

The desert and the mountaintop always remained important for Carmelites but the friars also responded to the call of the Church to evangelise the poor in the new cities of Europe. Contemplation was and is at the heart of the Carmelite vocation. Mendicant friars live this contemplative vocation in the midst of the people, whereas the hermits and the cloistered nuns live the same vocation in a different way. For all Carmelites, whether we live in the city or on the mountain, the journey through the desert, another way to express the contemplative path, is essential.

In the XI and XII centuries, the term "Pauperes Christi" (the poor ones of Christ) was often used for those who wished to serve Christ in and through the abandonment of goods and the embracing of poverty. These movements arose among lay people. The mendicant movement was a response to a particular situation in the Church. Francis and Dominic opted for a collective poverty for their new Orders. They brought together the best insights of the previous two centuries. The friars established themselves mostly in the cities, where there were acute social and moral problems. In 1247 the Carmelites joined this movement.

The foundation and essence of the consecrated life is the radical following of Jesus Christ. The evangelical counsels of poverty, chastity and obedience professed publicly in the Church are a radical form of witness to the following of Christ. They are *"above all a gift of the Most Holy Trinity"*[2], whose eternal and infinite love *"reaches the roots of one's being"* (VC, 18). When the vows are embraced with a generous commitment, the evangelical counsels contribute to the purification of the human heart and to the attainment of spiritual freedom. Religious are called to become conformed to Christ and a *"living memory of Jesus' way of life and way of acting"* (VC, 22). Far from taking religious out of the world, by the profession of the evangelical counsels they become a leaven for the transformation of the world and witness of the *"wonders that God accomplishes through human fragility"* (VC, 20).

Chastity, poverty and obedience are not virtues exclusive to consecrated people. All Christians are called to live in some way these evangelical counsels. The Consecrated Life is proposed as an alternative way of life in the Church. It is the vocation of all Christians to live in the world following the Gospel: the consecrated life is one way. Religious try, with more or less success, to create a different kind of world. Religious seek to offer an alternative vision of reality through the vows that they profess. The vows express a commitment to the person of Jesus Christ and are a way of participating in the mission of the Church by bearing witness to the Reign of God in this world. Religious are called to live this witness in a very ambiguous reality, in social settings that are constituted often by sinful structures that are locked in mortal combat with initiatives that promote a just relationship between human beings.

The three vows together form a unified way of following the poor, chaste and obedient Christ. By means of the vow of poverty, God frees the human heart from disordered attachments to material things. Our world has abundant resources for each and every human being but the way in which one part of humanity chooses to live means that the majority must live in poverty. When the rich countries give aid to the developing nations, they normally do so with many conditions, which condemn the latter to a never-ending cycle of poverty. The wealthy nations refuse to take the simple step of opening up their markets to the goods of these countries under the same conditions that they extend to their own goods. The rich nations often heavily subsidise their own goods making it impossible for developing nations to compete. These are structural sins, but there also exists a disordered relationship at an individual level. We must care for creation. All things have been created to be used, but it is very easy to become enslaved by them. Many peoples are living at such a level that the good things of the earth that sustain human life are not being renewed and this will have disastrous effects on future generations unless we each choose to live in this world as good stewards and not as rapacious masters.

Our relationship with material things must be purified during the journey in the desert, so that our hearts do not grasp onto these things. God will help us find our treasure in God alone and not in any created thing. In this experience we find that many things that have given us great pleasure in the past can become quite tasteless. This is true also for spiritual things. For example, prayer can be very pleasurable at a certain stage on the journey and the danger is that we can pray for the pleasure that we receive and not because prayer is the privileged means of communication with God. Often prayer will become arid and without any meaning for us. Through such experiences we lose the exaggerated dependence on our own feelings. God makes us capable of accepting reality as it is, and in this way we learn that things, even spiritual things, can never satisfy us fully. They may give us a momentary pleasure and then our heart looks around for the next thing. We learn that only God can fully satisfy the human heart. We learn this important lesson through experience and sometimes experience can be bitter.

Sometimes when we are experiencing the desert, it can seem that everything is going wrong, but God is at work deep within us, putting in order all our feelings and disordered desires. This experience is a blessing, even though it seems to be the opposite. The way in which we relate to God, to others and to the world around us changes. We can then understand those mysterious words of Jesus: *"the one who wants to save his life will lose it; but the one who is prepared to lose his life for love of me, will save it."* (Lc. 9,24). We begin to understand not only intellectually but also from the heart, because we have experienced the truth of the words. The vow of poverty is one means that God uses to liberate our heart so that we can be in a life giving relationship with God, with other people and with material things.

Certainly the vows demand a renunciation but the reason behind it is to free the heart in order to love. Living the vows as well as possible, leaves space for God to transform the human being in order to see as if with God's eyes and love as if with God's heart. There is no virtue in renunciation for its own sake; it is only valuable when it is to benefit other people. Think of athletes. They train very hard and the goal can seem very far away. It is difficult not to become disillusioned and think that it really is not worth all the struggle. However the desert is not always dry; at times we might be permitted to glimpse something of what is happening deep within us and this gives us new strength when we understand that God is liberating us so that we can love God and other people as our brothers and sisters, and to love the whole of creation as a divine gift for the whole of the human family.

The option for the poor requires a compassionate way of looking upon the world. It challenges us to evaluate our lifestyle, our ways of making decisions on a personal as well as an institutional level in terms of their impact on the poor. By means of a simple lifestyle, religious communities bear witness to and announce the Good News of God's Reign. Communities of consecrated men and women can make present in this world in a very concrete way an alternative way of living, which is a sign of God's Reign. A poor, humble and simple lifestyle is also a denunciation of the present systems of our world, because they go against the current. The poverty of the religious will challenge other people only if we allow ourselves to be challenged first of all. If we become prisoners of the lifestyle of our own societies and accept the customs and ways of thinking of the more privileged sectors, we religious will not serve anyone, neither the poor nor the rich and the wealthy can only be saved by becoming poor like Christ, who *"though he was rich, yet for your sake he became poor, so that by his poverty, you might become rich."* (2 Cor. 8.9).

Poverty in Carmel

Below is what the Carmelite Order says regarding poverty in some of our more important official documents.

The Carmelite Rule
- The first thing I require is for you to have a Prior, one of yourselves, who is to be chosen for the office by common consent, or that of the greater and maturer part of you. Each of the others must promise him obedience - of which, once promised, he must try to make his deed the true reflection - *and also chastity and the renunciation of ownership.* (art. 4)[3]
- None of the brothers must lay claim to anything as his own, but you are to possess everything in common; and each is to receive from the Prior-that is from the brother he appoints for the purpose- whatever befits his age and needs. (art. 12)
- You are to abstain from meat, except as a remedy for sickness or feebleness. But as, when you are on a journey, you more often than not have to beg your way, outside your own houses you may eat foodstuffs that have been cooked with meat, so as to avoid giving trouble to your hosts. At sea, however, meat may be eaten. (art. 17)[4]
- You must give yourselves to work of some kind, so that the devil may always find you busy; no idleness on your part must give him a chance to pierce the defences of your souls. In this respect you have both the teaching and the example of Saint Paul the Apostle, into whose mouth Christ put his own words. God made him preacher and teacher of faith and truth to the nations: with him as your teacher you cannot go astray. We lived among you, he said, labouring and weary, toiling night and day so as not to be a burden to any of you; not because we had no

power to do otherwise but so as to give you, in your own selves, as an example you might imitate. For the charge we gave you when we were with you was this: that whoever is not willing to work should not be allowed to eat either. For we have heard that there are certain restless idlers among you. We charge people of this kind, and implore them in the name of the Lord Jesus Christ, that they earn their own bread by silent toil. This is the way of holiness and goodness: see that you follow it. (art. 20)

Constitutions of the Friars
- *Const. 24* – Finally, this way of being "in the midst of the people" is a sign and a prophetic witness of new relationships of fraternity and friendship among men and women everywhere. It is a prophetic message of justice and peace in society and among peoples. As an integral part of the Good News, this prophecy must be fulfilled through active commitment to the transformation of sinful systems and structures into grace-filled systems and structures. It is also an expression of "the choice to share in the lives of "the little ones" (*"minores"*) of history, so that we may speak a word of hope and of salvation from their midst - more by our life than by our words." This option flows naturally from our profession of poverty in a mendicant fraternity, and is in keeping with our allegiance to Christ Jesus, lived out also through allegiance to the poor and to those in whom the face of our Lord is reflected in a preferential way.[5]

- *Const. 50* – Jesus Christ the poor man, was born and lived in lowliness. During his life on earth, he chose to be deprived of all worldly riches,[6] power and prestige.[7] He took the form of a slave, becoming as human beings are,[8] and identified with the "little ones" and with the poor.[9] He shared all of his life with his disciples;[10] he shared his Father's plans,[11] his mission,[12] his prayer.[13] In this way, he became not only their master, but their friend and brother.[14] On the cross, in keeping with the Father's plan, Jesus experienced absolute nakedness and radical poverty. From the cross he gave himself up completely, for the sake of humanity. Rich though he was, Jesus became poor for us, so that, through his poverty, we might be made rich.[15]
- *Const. 52* – As we follow Jesus and take as our model the life of the primitive Church, we too wish to embrace willingly the gift of the evangelical counsel of poverty, by our vow to hold all things in common, and by declaring that no object belongs to any of us personally. We believe that all we have is gift, and that all we have - all the spiritual, material, and cultural goods that are obtained by our labour - must be freely returned, in whatever way can best serve the good of the Church and of our Order, for the human and social development of all.
- *Const. 53* – Poverty is a complex and ambiguous reality. When it is the absence of the necessary means for survival, resulting from injustice or personal and social sin, it is an evil. But it can

also be a Gospel form of life adopted by those who trust in God alone, sharing all their possessions, identifying with the poor in a spirit of solidarity, renouncing all desire for dominion or self-sufficiency. In contemplation, we internalise the authentic attitude of poverty, which is a deep process of inner self-emptying through which we become less and less in control of our own activity and ideas, of our virtues and of our ambitions, as we open ourselves to God's action. In this way, we become truly poor as Christ was poor, even to the point of not owning the poverty we have chosen in this process by which God's love empties us.

- *Const. 54* – Thus, we who freely chose poverty as our evangelical lifestyle feel called by the Gospel and by the Church to awaken people's consciences to the problems of destitution, hunger and social injustice. We shall accomplish this purpose if - first and foremost - our own poverty witnesses to the human meaning of work as a means of sustaining life and as service to others; if we undertake to study and to understand the economic, social and moral causes of that poverty which stems from injustice; if we use our possessions with restraint and simplicity, making them available to others, even free of charge, in the service of the human and spiritual development of our fellow men and women; and, finally, if we engage in healthy and balanced discernment with regard to the ways in which we are present among the people, choosing ways which foster the liberation and the integral development of human beings.

- *Const. 58* – Let us remember that in our time the best way to make manifest our vow of poverty is to faithfully fulfil the common law of work. Let us, therefore, embrace with enthusiasm the precept of the Rule, which invites us to work assiduously, for we know that by our toil we co-operate in God's work of creation and, at the same time, develop our own personalities; by our active charity we assist our confreres, and all others; and we contribute to the good of the Order. Moreover, we perpetuate the dignity Jesus gave to work - for he never disdained manual labour - and we follow the example of the Blessed Virgin Mary, whose life on earth was full of ordinary concerns and work.
- *Const. 110* – Christ did not bring about the salvation of the human race as an outsider or as a stranger to the history of the world. On the contrary, he identified both with his people and with the whole human race. Those who "claim to be followers of Christ must heed his call, especially when he says: "I was hungry and you gave me to eat; I was thirsty and you gave me to drink; I was a stranger and you welcomed me; I was naked and you clothed me; I was sick and you visited me; I was in prison and you came to me"[16]
- *Const.111* – We live in a world full of injustice and disquiet. It is our duty to contribute to the search for an understanding of the causes of

these evils; to be in solidarity with the sufferings of those who are marginalized; to share in their struggle for justice and peace; and to fight for their total liberation, helping them to fulfil their desire for a decent life.
- *Const. 112* – The poor, the "little ones" (*minores*), constitute the vast majority of the world population. Their complex problems are linked and, to a large extent, are caused by current international relations and, more directly, by the economic and political systems which govern our world today. We cannot turn a deaf ear to the cry of the oppressed who plead for justice.
- *Const. 113* – We must hear and interpret reality from the perspective of the poor - of those who are oppressed by the economic and political systems which today govern humanity. Their problems are many, and we must set priorities in responding to them. In this way, we shall rediscover the Gospel as good news, and Jesus Christ as the liberator from all forms of oppression.
- *Const. 114* – Social reality challenges us. Attentive to the cry of the poor, and faithful to the Gospel, we must take our stand with them, making an option for the "little ones". "There is a growing desire within the Order to choose solidarity with the "little ones" of history, to bring to our brothers and sisters a word of hope and salvation from their midst, more by our lives than by our words... We recommend this option for the poor, because it is in keeping with the charism of the Order, which can be

summarised as 'a life in allegiance to Jesus Christ'; allegiance to Jesus also means allegiance to the poor and to those in whom the face of Christ is mirrored preferentially.
- *Const. 115* – Our Elijan inspiration, which our prophetic charism is founded on, calls us to walk with the "little ones" along the paths the prophet travelled in his time - along the path of justice, opposing false ideologies and moving towards a concrete experience of the true living God; along the path of solidarity, defending the victims of injustice and taking their part; along the path of mysticism, struggling to restore to the poor faith in themselves by renewing their awareness that God is on their side.
- *Const. 116* – To prepare and educate ourselves so that we may take on "the circumstances of the poor" in an evangelical manner, we propose to re-read the Bible, also from the perspective of the poor, of the oppressed and of the marginalized; to consider the Christian principles of justice and peace as an integral part of our formation at every level; to immerse ourselves in the circumstances of the poor; to use the tools of social analysis, in the light of faith, as a means to discover the presence of sin incarnated in certain political, socio-economic and cultural structures; to defend and to encourage even the smallest traces of vitality.

The Ratio Institutionis Vitae Carmelitanae
- *RIVC 5* – The Father - who, through the action of the Holy Spirit, calls us to a spiritual

experience of deep attraction to and love for Jesus Christ the chaste, poor and obedient One - is the source and the goal of religious life, and therefore of Carmelite life. Through the Holy Spirit, the Father consecrates us, transforms us and conforms us to the image of Christ, guiding us to communion with himself and with our brothers and sisters.

As individuals and as communities, we in turn choose Jesus as the one Lord and Saviour of our lives. We commit ourselves to a journey of gradual and progressive conversion encompassing every aspect of life, allowing ourselves to be conformed to Jesus by the action of the Spirit and to come to union with God.

- *RIVC 9* – The evangelical counsels of obedience, poverty and chastity, publicly professed, are a concrete and radical way of following Christ. They are "above all a gift of the Holy Trinity,"[17] whose eternal and infinite love touches "the very root of our being."[18]

  When they are embraced with the generous commitment which flows from love, the evangelical counsels contribute to purification of the heart and to spiritual freedom. By means of the evangelical counsels, the Holy Spirit gradually transforms us and conforms us to Christ. We become "a living memorial of Jesus' way of living and acting."[19]

  Far from becoming estranged from the world by the profession of the evangelical counsels, we become a leaven for the transformation of the world, and we bear witness to "the marvels wrought by God in... the frail humanity of those who are called."[20]

- *RIVC 43* – The contemplative dimension of Carmelite life allows us to recognise God's action in creation and in history. This free gift challenges us to commit ourselves to the working out of God's plan for the world. The authentic contemplative journey allows us to discover our own frailty, our weakness, our poverty - in a word, the nothingness of human nature: all is grace. Through this experience, we grow in solidarity with those who live in situations of deprivation and injustice. As we allow ourselves to be challenged by the poor and by the oppressed, we are gradually transformed, and we begin to see the world with God's eyes and to love the world with his heart.[21] With God, we hear the cry of the poor,[22] and we strive to share the Divine solicitude, concern, and compassion for the poorest and the least.

This moves us to speak out prophetically in the face of the excesses of individualism and subjectivism which we see in today's mentality - in the face of the many forms of injustice and oppression of individuals and of peoples.

Commitment to justice, peace and the safeguarding of creation is not an option. It is an urgent challenge, to which contemplative and prophetic Carmelite communities - following the example of Elijah[23] and of Mary[24] - must respond, speaking out in explicit defence of the truth and of the divine plan for humanity and for creation as a whole. Our community lifestyle is in itself such a statement: it is founded on just and peaceful relations, according to the plan outlined in the Rule, which our tradition traces back to the experience of Elijah, who founded on Mount Carmel a community where justice and peace dwell.[25]

What does poverty say to Carmel now?

In the Carmelite Rule, which is the foundational document giving rise to all the different forms of Carmelite life, we are told that, like all those who seek to live a Christian life, we must live in allegiance to Jesus Christ. To do so means to be like him and assume his poor and fraternal style of life (Mk. 3, 14) It also means to imitate him when faced with the difficulties and privations of life (Lk. 22, 28), and finally to follow him to Calvary (Mk. 15, 41). We are to identify ourselves with Christ to the point of saying: "*I live, now not I, but it is Christ who lives in me!*" (Gal. 2, 20)

The saints of Carmel have consistently stressed poverty as a spiritual value by means of which we come to realise our own need for God. According to St. John of the Cross, one of the results of dark contemplation is precisely the coming to know intimately one's own poverty and misery (Dark Night 2, 6, 4). He tells us that,

> *All the wealth and glory of creation compared to the wealth that is God is utter poverty and misery in the Lord's sight.*

> *The person who loves and possesses these things is completely poor and miserable before God and will be unable to attain the richness and glory of transformation in God.*[26]

St. Thérèse of Lisieux had a profound understanding of her own poverty. She knew that she could do nothing and so she trusted totally in the power of God to bring her to the summit of Mount Carmel. Edith Stein and Titus Brandsma have given us the powerful example of their own life and death. Titus had an important job and led a very busy life. Despite all that, he was well known for having time for everyone. Finally he had to let go of everything when he was imprisoned and sent to Dachau, the infamous concentration camp, where he met his death with peacefulness and forgiveness for his torturers. In his famous poem we see that in his experience of utter poverty, Titus experienced a greater closeness with Christ than ever before:

> *Leave me here freely alone,*
> *In cell where never sunlight shone,*
> *Should no one ever speak to me,*
> *This golden silence makes me free!*
>
> *For though alone, I have no fear;*
> *Never wert Thou, O Lord, so near.*
> *Sweet Jesus, please abide with me;*
> *My deepest peace I find in Thee.*[27]

The first Carmelite hermits went to Albert of Jerusalem to receive from him direction for their lives and he specifically states in the "Formula

Vitae" that he based himself on the proposal which they themselves had brought to him. They are to prepare themselves for a battle by putting on the armour of Christ. Albert in chapter 19 of the Rule details what this armour is:

> *Your loins are to be girt with chastity, your breast fortified by holy meditations, for as Scripture has it, holy meditation will save you. Put on holiness as your breastplate, and it will enable you to love the Lord your God with all your heart and soul and strength, and your neighbour as yourself. Faith must be your shield on all occasions, and with it you will be able to quench all the flaming missiles of the wicked one: there can be no pleasing God without faith; and the victory lies in this-your faith. On your head set the helmet of salvation, and so be sure of deliverance by our only Saviour, who sets his own free from their sins. The sword of the spirit, the word of God, must abound in your mouths and hearts. Let all you do have the Lord's word for accompaniment.*

The desert was often considered to be the stronghold of Satan and hermits were considered to be in the forefront of the battle against evil. They went out into the desert not for a quiet life away from it all but in order to take part in this battle. They discovered that the battle was mostly interior against their own selfishness or false self that was always ready to spoil even the best of intentions. In the desert the hermits experienced their own poverty. They came to realise that without the help of God, they could do nothing.

The Rule is an ancient document that has something to say to each succeeding generation. In the 21st century we too have a battle to fight and we too need to be protected by the same armour that the first Carmelites donned. When the hermits left Mount Carmel for Europe, they brought with them the desert of Carmel, no longer a geographical place, but now an expression of the charism. They rediscovered the desert when they assumed the mendicant life, in the midst of the poor in the great cities of Europe. The Carmelite vocation takes us on a journey through the desert, just like our father Elijah. At times we may feel that we cannot win. We may have struggled for many years in various apostolates and not seen much fruit. We may have tried for many years to overcome the selfishness and rebellion that lurks in every human heart. God hears the cry of the poor and asks us to hear it too but what can we do? Despite our best efforts, it can seem that the rich get richer and the poor get poorer. Through the experience of the desert, we come to realise our own poverty, the fact that of ourselves we can accomplish nothing. The Kingdom of God is a gift not something that we can force by our good deeds. Perhaps like Elijah we may realise that we are no better than our ancestors (I Kings 19,4) and that we have been adding to the problem instead of alleviating it. If we lie down under the nearest bush and refuse to carry on, we too will receive a visit from an angel. This being will not have six wings and be surrounded by light but will look very ordinary, God uses anyone and anything to convey a message to us. The message is that we must get up and eat lest the journey be too long. (I Kings 19,7) The daily food for our journey we receive is the Eucharist and our Carmelite tradition. Like the Prophet Elijah we must go on a long journey. We must never cease what we have been called to do but in and through all things we must seek the face of the living God. Elijah received a great surprise when he reached Mount Horeb for God was not in the earthquake, or in the mighty wind or in the great fire. Instead Elijah encountered God in a way that nothing had prepared him for, in the sound of sheer silence. (I Kings 19,12)

In our service of the poor, we too must come to realise that God's work is often accomplished in seemingly very quiet ways. Perhaps we wish that we could see with our own eyes what Our Lady prophesied: *the poor he has filled with good things and the rich he has sent empty away.* (Lk. 1, 53) However, we do not see that. Perhaps we need to adjust our way of seeing so that we begin to see as God sees and love as God loves. (cf. Constitutions of the Friars 15). In our journey through the desert we are stripped of all our pretensions so that we can truly accomplish the Lord's will and not our own.

Poverty can be degrading and is for millions of our brothers and sisters throughout the world. It is this poverty against which we must never cease to struggle so that every human being might be able to live a decent life. However, people need more than material things. Pope Benedict XVI, in his first encyclical, *Deus Caritas Est*, writes

> *Seeing with the eyes of Christ, I can give to others much more than their outward necessities; I can give them the look of love which they crave… Only my readiness to encounter my neighbour and to show him love makes me sensitive to God as well (art. 18).*

Poverty as a spiritual value, can be taken as a synonym for humility, by means of which we realise our own nothingness, that all is grace, and that we must depend utterly on God who clothes the flowers of the field in a way that not even Solomon in all his glory was arrayed. (Lk. 12, 27)

Endnotes

1. For more information on this and other United Nations projects, see the Carmelite NGO website – *www.carmelitengo.org*.
2. *Vita Consacrata*, 20. This is the document written by Pope John Paul II in 1994 after the Episcopal Synod on the Consecrated Life. Hereinafter it is referred to as VC.
3. The words *"and also chastity and the renunciation of ownership"* were added to St. Albert's original "formula vitae" by Pope Innocent IV in 1247 in order to bring the lay hermits into line with other mendicant friars and therefore make them officially religious.
4. Articles 12 and 17 were added by Pope Innocent IV for the above reason.
5. This is a quote from the final message of a meeting of the Order (the General Congregation) from 1980.
6. Luke 9:58.
7. John 6:15; 5:41.
8. Phil 2:7.
9. Matt 25:40.
10. John 1:39.
11. John 15: 15.
12. Matt 10.
13. Luke 11:1-4.

14 Heb 2:11; Rom 8:29.
15 2 Cor 8:9.
16 Matt 25:35-36.
17 VC, 20.
18 VC, 18.
19 VC, 22.
20 VC, 20.
21 Cf. Constitutions of the Friars, 15.
22 Cf. Ex. 3, 7.
23 Cf. I Kings 21.
24 Cf. Lk. 1, 46. 55.
25 Cf. *Instituto Primorum Monachorum*, 3, 3, 5.
26 Ascent I, 4, 7. This translation is taken from K. KAVANAUGH and O. RODRIGUEZ, *The Collected Works of St. John of the Cross* (Washington DC, ICS Publications, 1991), p. 126.
27 The whole poem can be found published in various places including, J. REES, *Titus Brandsma. A Modern Martyr*, (Sidgwick & Jackson, London, 1971), p. 122.

OUR MENDICANT TRADITION

Our Inheritance

All Carmelites look back to the founding experience of the hermits on Mount Carmel. We do not know how long they had lived there or who they were. When did they decide to make obedience to the hermit named simply as "B" in the Rule and which our rich tradition fills out as Brocard? How long did they live simply under obedience to Brocard or whatever he was called? Eventually they decided to ask Albert, the Patriarch of Jerusalem, to write for them some sort of guide for their way of life. We know that he complied some time between 1206 and 1214 and we call what he gave to the hermits the "Formula Vitae" or formula for living.

St. Albert specifically writes that he is basing his guide for the hermits' life on their proposal:

> *It is to me, however, that you have come for a rule of life in keeping with your avowed purpose, a rule you may hold fast to henceforward.*

The first Carmelites were hermits and so the "rule of life" is written for the eremitical life. In about 40 years the group had joined the new mendicant movement spearheaded by the Dominicans and

Franciscans. The growing Carmelite community wanted to move into the new cities and work with the greatly increasing number of urban poor. We need not go into why they wanted to do so. However in 1247 the "formula vitae" was approved by Pope Innocent IV with certain modifications designed to make the Carmelite life suitable for the cities. These modifications were made following the suggestions by two Dominicans appointed by the Pope to examine the document before its approval as a Rule. With the approval of the Pope, the formula vitae became an official Rule of the Church.

It took the Carmelites some time to adapt to the new way of life as mendicant friars. One of the earliest existing Carmelite documents is that of the former Prior General, Nicholas the Gaul, Ignea Sagitta, the Flaming Arrow. In this letter the Prior General was complaining about so many young friars rushing into active apostolates without adequate preparation and so damaging themselves and others. The theological motto of the Dominicans is to share with others the fruit of their contemplation. The Carmelites wanted to teach others how to contemplate, in the sense of doing what we can to prepare ourselves to receive God's gift when and if God chooses to give it to us. In order to be faithful to this vocation, the Carmelite must have a strong commitment to prayer and to the work of transformation. To be so taken up with outside activity as to forget our primary relationship with God is to invite disaster and be unfaithful to our vocation.

The Carmelites became mendicants *as Carmelites* and did not simply forget all that they had inherited from their eremitical predecessors on Mount Carmel. Of course a part of our Family remains monastic, that is the cloistered nuns, and we also have several communities of hermits around the world. All of the reform movements throughout the history of the Order harked back to the idealised life of the hermits on Mount Carmel and the values of solitude, silence and contemplation. Our past with its values is our inheritance and is part of our lives. The mingling of the eremitical with the mendicant gives the particular flavour to the Carmelite soup that we know and love. There are many other good soups but it is the Carmelite soup that God chooses to give us the nourishment we need. The Carmelite soup, as I call it, or perhaps the Carmelite salad, are down to earth ways of describing the charism. Soups and salads differ according to the ingredients employed. Sometimes similar ingredients are used but the amount of each makes the difference.

Our Mendicant Inheritance: Mobility

Due to the decision of those early Carmelites to join the mendicant movement, the Order has received a specific inheritance. Before the advent of the mendicant Orders, the religious life manifested itself fundamentally in monasticism and the life of canons in community. These models established a particular relationship with the world and required stability to a place. For the mendicant the only stability is our obedience. We are not itinerants moving around at our own whim but by our vow of obedience, we pledge ourselves to be available for the mission of our Order. We have no lasting city. We are appointed to a community and when there is another need we can be asked to move in order to respond to that need. This is not the slavish doing of someone else's will but listening to the will of God, which comes to us through a need expressed by a religious superior.

We cannot afford to build little empires because at some point we will be asked to leave them behind, even if it is only at death, and it is better to be accustomed to letting go by the time we reach that point. The evangelical mendicant ideal urges us to be ever on a journey and to cultivate a docility to divine providence. Stability and monastic autonomy emerged from the feudal system of medieval Europe. Mendicants opt for mobility and availability for God's will. It is not sufficient to attract people to our churches or whatever we have; we must go out from our sanctuaries and go to new market places. When we go to new places, we have to learn the language of the people, otherwise we will not be able to communicate. This is the case for learning a modern language but also refers to the ability to communicate with the people of today. It is useless to talk to the people of tomorrow in the language of yesterday. We need not try to talk like young people, which can sound ridiculous, but it is good to be aware of how we are communicating or not. What do we communicate to people by the way we live? Have we built or are we trying to build a little empire for ourselves? This is often very difficult for us to see but to others it tends to be much clearer.

The Battle

In our Rule, St. Albert, citing the first letter of Peter, tells us to put on the armour of God. The reason is that we have a fierce battle to engage in and it would be extremely foolish to forget that. In medieval times this battle was pictured as one against demons. Nowadays the same battle tends to be pictured in a different way: the battle field is the human heart and the combatants are the new person, recreated in the image of Christ, and the false self. This latter is the selfishness that lurks in every human heart, always ready to engulf the individual. The false self is very, very subtle and can easily adapt itself to any way of life. If the false self is unrestrained, it is like a lion going about looking for someone to eat (1Pet 5,8). Those who take the Christian life seriously usually restrain the false self somewhat but gradually these restraints can become very loose unless we are very careful. The false self does not object at all to our choice of living the consecrated life. While our eyes are on Jesus Christ and our hearts full of love for him, the false self, which will remain part of us till we take our last breath, is busy looking for opportunities for itself. How big a part the false self will play in our lives will depend on whether we take it seriously and seek to limit its influence upon us. The false self is very happy as a Carmelite because there are innumerable opportunities for selfishness in the consecrated way of life.

Usually we have to hide our selfishness from ourselves because we like to think that we are very generous and faithful followers of Christ. The false self inserts itself in our good works and gradually spoils our motivation, if we allow it do so. So brick by brick I begin to build my little empire where the false self rules.

The false self can insinuate itself into every area of our life. It is rather like one bad apple that slowly affects all the other apples in the barrel with its decay. We must seek to be aware of its presence and how it makes itself felt in our lives. We must use the weapons given us by God - faith, prayer, the sacraments etc. The values of the consecrated life and the Carmelite life in particular are also very important weapons against the false self. We can pay lip service to these values while our hearts might in fact follow other values.

Our feelings, when we are under stress or being challenged, will tell us much about where our heart really is. I invite you to look inside yourself and ask yourself what your real values are. Do you think that your brothers and sisters in community would agree with your judgement? Are you available for the mission of the Order or only for the mission you have chosen for yourself? Is the

Order available for the mission of the Church, which is to carry on throughout the ages the mission of Christ? Are we so concerned as Provinces or as Congregations to build up our corporate empires that we have no possibility of changing in order to respond to changing needs?

The healthy tension

We are inheritors of the choice our Carmelite predecessors made to join the mendicant movement. When they made that choice they received a mission from Christ through the Church to an active apostolate. However, in Carmel there is always a tension, which hopefully is healthy and keeps us in balance between the active ministry and the life of prayer. The Carmelite has in his or her soul a certain nostalgia for the desert and for the mountains. We stress contemplation as our core value in the following of Christ. The active apostolate can at times be exhausting but also very often it can be very rewarding on the level of how we feel. Intimacy with God is the essential motor for any active apostolate in order for it to be in tune with the mind and heart of Christ. The false self is always ready to move in and take over an apostolate if Christ is not the centre of our lives. The false self will also give us good reasons to escape from our duty in order to take care of ourselves. The false self will never urge us to engage in a real encounter with the Lord but will seek even to utilise prayer for its own purposes.

What is Carmel's Mission?

Prophetic service is an essential element of the Carmelite charism. It is an essential ingredient in the Carmelite soup that nourishes us all. Without this ingredient, it would be a different soup, which would not give us who are called to Carmel the nourishment we need. Every Carmelite is called to service whether the service takes place in a favela in Brazil or within the walls of a monastery. The mission might be to work in a parish or a school or it might be to lie on a sick bed and call forth love from others. This is an element that comes originally from the choice that the Carmelite hermits made more than 800 years ago to join the mendicant movement. They left Mount Carmel in a physical sense, although they always carried it in their heart, and reconstituted it in the new cities of Europe in the midst of the people, and especially among the new urban poor.

What makes a particular service Carmelite? Many people work with the poor or the sick or in parishes but I believe that the Franciscan form of service tastes different from the Dominican form or the Carmelite form. I am not saying one is better than another; it is just different. The Carmelite soup is the one I like; it is the one that God knows will give me the strength for the journey each of us must undertake, like our father Elijah, to the mountain of God.

So, what lies at the heart of all true Carmelite service? What is it that makes a particular work "Carmelite"? Does it matter? I believe it does. We have been called to Carmel and we are most faithful to God when we are faithful to what God is asking of us. Remember the story that Jesus told of the two sons who were both asked to work in the fields. The first one said "yes, of course" but he did not go; the second refused to go but in the end he did as he was asked (Mt. 21, 28-31). There is a critical difference between "working for God" and "doing God's work". The first, "working for God", means to do in general what we think God is probably asking of us. It is amazing how often God's will coincides with what we want to do or have already decided to do. The second "doing God's work" means to really do what God is asking of us, which might be quite different. There are various ways that we can seek to escape doing what God is really asking of us and instead we can impose our own will on that of God. Therefore we should not simply assume that we are doing God's work. We need to discern God's will, which is not easy.

The way we do God's work above all is to be faithful to our Carmelite vocation. The essential elements of Carmel are well known: we live in allegiance to Jesus Christ, inspired by the example of the Prophet Elijah and Mary, the mother of Jesus; we emphasise the values of prophetic service, fraternity and prayer; the core value is contemplation, by means of which we gradually are transformed in Christ to become a new creation, seeing with the eyes of God and loving with the heart of God.

An element of our charism that has not been much developed is the place that St. Paul has in our Rule. He is much quoted in the Rule and he is very clearly presented to Carmelites as a model for work. The Rule, chapter 20 says this:

> *There is work to be done by you, so that the devil may always find you occupied; no idleness on your part must give him a chance to pierce the defences of your souls. In this respect you have both the teaching and example of St. Paul the Apostle, into whose mouth Christ put his own words. God made him preacher and teacher of faith and truth to the nations: with him as your leader you cannot go astray.*

It goes on to quote from the second letter to the Thessalonians about imitating Paul in the way he worked (2 Th 3,7-13).

Kees Waaijman, in his book, *The Mystical Space of Carmel*,[1] reflects on why the example of St. Paul is so strongly underlined in the Rule. His answer is that Paul gives the example of how Christians must work in this world while being directed towards the End times. In Genesis, work is seen as a punishment imposed on human beings by God. (3, 17-19). In Ecclesiastes it is considered vexation and vanity (2, 18-23). To the psalmist of psalm 104, work is a way of joining God in creating things based on God's wisdom (v.23-24). Psalm 8 views human beings as God's deputies. Humanity manages creation on God's behalf and in the name of God. Human labour is seen from a variety of perspectives. In Thessalonica, Paul met a problem concerning some people who were so convinced that the End was imminent that they stopped working and interfered with everyone else. He strongly tells the Christians in that city, and us, that work is still very important. We are not to work to build up our own little kingdom; instead our work must be to prepare for the coming Reign of God.

The question of what is the motive for our work emerges from this idea of work in the Rule. Paul's work was directed to building up the Body of Christ. In order not to be a burden and not to give his enemies an opportunity to lead people astray, he refused to take what was his right as an emissary of the Gospel and so he worked night and day. Most religious work very hard but what are the underlying motives?

Are we always directed by pure motives? I do not think that any one of us will have completely pure motives until after the general resurrection. Until then we have to deal with mixed motives. It is very important to be aware of this fact so that we can be on our guard and not assume that our work is for the Kingdom of God. Remember the story in the synoptic Gospels where Jesus asks his disciples about the opinion of the people. The disciples tell Jesus some of the rumours going around among the people. I imagine that they were laughing as they talked. Then Jesus became serious and asked them what they thought: "*And you, who do you say that I am?*" Peter spoke up for them all and declared that he was the long-awaited Messiah. (Mk 8, 27-30; Mt. 16,13-16; Lk 9,18ff). Peter was theologically correct. Jesus is the Messiah. However, when Jesus went on to explain what was the mission of the Messiah, Peter very strongly rejected the explanation. What is the Kingdom of God and what does it mean to work for the coming of the

Kingdom? It is important not to assume too quickly that we know the answer. We must learn slowly and gradually from Jesus. Without a serious commitment to prayer in the sense of an encounter with Jesus Christ, we can be absolutely sure that we will have the wrong answer! Remember what Jesus said to Peter when the disciple wanted to dissuade him from his mission.

The core value of Carmel that holds all the other values together is of course contemplation. It is like the recipe we follow to make the Carmelite soup; if we do not follow the recipe, we will end up with something completely different. The mission of Carmel in the Church is made up of all the values we have mentioned put together. However we seek to live all these values from a contemplative perspective. Mary and Elijah are immensely rich characters but we look at them through the glasses of contemplation.

In pastoral situations there are innumerable things to do and we could very easily get caught up in a whirl of activity and lose sight of our goal, which is to play our part in continuing Christ's mission on earth until he comes again. Cultivating a silent heart is important in order that our activity comes from a still point within us. Otherwise we might just be adding empty noise to a very noisy world. We must seek to silence all the noise within us (the commentaries and the judgements on others that go on in our heads; our inability to listen because we are so interested in the conversations taking place with ourselves). As we allow all the internal noise to die away, we can begin to really hear those to whom we minister without distortion and respond to their real needs, not what we think they need.

As Carmelites we are called to become contemplatives. To be a contemplative does not mean to live a particular style of life but describes a level of intimacy with God. The goal of the contemplative journey is to become mature friends of Jesus Christ to such a degree that his values become our values and we begin to see with God's eyes and love with God's heart. When God gazes on the world, God sees beyond the externals; God sees the motivation of the human heart. A contemplative can really hear what other people are saying. Often we tend to impose our own ideas on others because we are incapable of hearing them. We can be very generous in working for God, but fail to understand what God is actually asking of us. Authentic contemplation must find expression in a commitment to serve others in some manner and this service will be according to the mind and heart of God ("doing God's work").

The mission of the mendicants is fundamentally to proclaim the Gospel of Jesus Christ. Whatever our particular apostolate may be, it must in some way come under the banner of bringing the Good News to others. In order to be faithful to our mission, we must proclaim the Gospel firstly with our lives before we can do so with our lips. By our fraternal lives we bear witness to the truth of the Gospel. There is a saying in English, the proof of the pudding is in the eating - in other words, do not tell me how good the pudding is, let me taste it and I will tell you. So the authenticity of your words can be seen only in the way you live.

The mendicant community

Community is a wonderful sign that the love of God can perform miracles in the hearts of human beings. It proclaims the truth of the Gospel and is an integral part of our mission. We are all aware of the beautiful theory of community and the pleasure it can be to live in a good community but we are no doubt equally aware of the drawbacks of community. At times it is not easy to live in community because it is made up of imperfect human beings who hopefully are all on the spiritual journey and who can support one another to arrive at the goal for which we were all created. Nevertheless they are imperfect human beings who are all seeking happiness in ways that will never fully satisfy them. These ways clash from time to time because until the transformation process has reached a certain point of maturity, we are all seeking infinite esteem and affection, security and control, which of course we cannot all have, and therefore we experience personality clashes.

When we make profession, we commit ourselves to a group of real people who are fundamentally good but who are imperfect. We commit ourselves to throw in our lot with these people. We are asked to love our neighbour who is a real flesh and blood human being with feelings, who does not always react the way we expect. It is easy to love another human being in theory but more difficult to do so in practice. It is easy to love the entire human race but more difficult to love a real person. Perhaps we should thank God that we get on as well in community as we do. Human relationships are not at all easy. We should thank God that the companions on our journey are mostly people who are trying their best to live the Gospel as they see it, even though we may find that difficult to believe at times.

It can be very tempting to try to escape the demands placed on us by living in community. We can be very good at serving those outside community from a position of superiority, but with those who live in the same house, who share our table, the recreation room and perhaps also the apostolate, there can be friction. This friction is the way God smoothes the rough edges of our personality and deepens the process of purification and transformation. God is making a masterpiece of our lives and the tools God often uses are our brothers and sisters. We should thank these brothers and sisters of ours for helping us become what God is creating us to be.

We believe that a vocation comes from God but we must admit that mixed in with a divine call is the human element. So we find all sorts of people in religious communities. Perhaps some should never have become religious as they seem to be unsuited to community life; others have been embittered by the harsh experiences of everyday life and are never really happy no matter how many good things happen to them; others are suffering under various kinds of illnesses or addictions; others are trying their best to respond to what they believe God is asking of them and go wherever they are asked to go. Like everyone else they are limited, make mistakes, commit sin and so on.

A group of religious is a microcosm of the Church and the world. A vital part of the human response to a vocation is an acceptance of these concrete people with all their faults and failings. When we make our profession in the Order we take on community as an integral part of our vocation. This means that we have thrown in our lot with this group for better for worse, for richer for poorer, in sickness and in health till death do us part.

The celebration of the Eucharist and communal listening to the Word of God are great helps to build up community. The Eucharist is the celebration of the community but also forms community and so it deserves serious preparation. It transforms individuals into community and then sends us out to live the Gospel in daily life. Unfortunately the Eucharist can also be divisive within a community if too much attention is put on externals and too little paid to the heart of the matter.

The movement in the Rule from the individual cells to the chapel each day is a symbol of the effort needed constantly to go out of oneself in order to meet others and with them make community. Fraternity is a prophetic sign that it is possible to live in communion even though one has to pay the price.

Prayer can be used to boost our own ego instead of being an opening to the purifying and healing action of God but that danger is not a reason to give up prayer either as individuals or as communities. St. Teresa of Avila said that, with regard to prayer, we need to have a very determined determination to keep going and never give up. Each one of us is responsible for the health of the community. Being prayerful does not necessarily mean saying many prayers but allowing our prayer to change us and how we relate to others.

The rediscovery of Lectio Divina as a method of prayer has been very important for the whole Church and so also for the Order. One possible step of Lectio Divina is to share one's ideas on a text of Scripture with others but that is most certainly not the goal. The goal of Lectio is contemplation, which is a mature relationship with God in Jesus Christ in which our limited human ways of thinking, loving and acting are transformed into divine ways. Discussion of a text of Scripture and trying to apply it to the life of a community can be very helpful but much more powerful is sharing the experience of silence together in which all desire the presence and action of God within the community. Lectio Divina is very useful in communities but it is important not to stop the process less than half way.

In the midst of the poor

The mendicant movement arose as a gift of the Holy Spirit to the Church and the world at a time of great social upheaval. More and more people were moving from the countryside into the cities, rather like our own days, with the same result, a huge increase in the urban poor. When Pope Innocent IV approved the Formula Vitae of St.

Albert, and so made it an official Rule of the Church, the Pope made some small but significant changes to allow the Carmelite hermits to join the new mendicant movement. He gave the Carmelites permission to make foundations where they were given *"a site suitable and convenient for the observance proper to your Order."* (Rule 5).

Very quickly the Order began to make foundations in the midst of the poor and to share with them their joy and hope, grief and anguish. Living among the poor, we try to say to them that God is indeed present and that humanity's struggle is especially close to His heart. We try to show the love of God with our lives and not only with our lips.

Questions for Personal Reflection
1. What elements of mendicant spirituality appeal most to you?
2. How do you keep all the values of the Carmelite life in balance?
3. Can you discern when your false self tries to assert itself? In what ways?

Questions for Group Reflection
1. What values from the mendicant tradition do you find most helpful for the present situation of the Carmelite Family where you are?
2. Can you think of ways in which the false self might affect the living out of our values?
3. What might give more flavour to the Carmelite soup?

Endnotes

1 *The Mystical Space of Carmel. A Commentary on the Carmelite Rule*, (The Fiery Arrow Collection, Peeters, Leuven,1999), p. 205-210. Cf. BRUNO SECONDIN, *La Règle du Carmel. Un projet spiritual pour aujourd'hui* (Collection Grands Carmes, Éditions Parole et Silence, France, 2004), p. 171-187.